CHRISTIAN MARRIAGE
IN
CRISIS

Christian Marriage in Crisis

by David Phypers

A ministry of World Vision

MARC
EUROPE

British Library Cataloguing in Publication Data

Phypers, David
    Christian marriage in crisis.
    1. Marriage—Religious aspects—Christianity
    I. Title
    261.8′3581   BT706

    ISBN 0–947697–13–6

MARC Europe is an integral part of World Vision, an international Christian humanitarian organisation. MARC's object is to assist Christian leaders with factual information, surveys, management skills, strategic planning and other tools for evangelism. We also publish and distribute related books on mission, church growth, management, spiritual maturity and other topics.

To my dear wife, Margaret,
my companion and suitable helper,
without whose constant support
the writing of this book would
have been impossible.

Other books by David Phypers (Co-author with Donald Bridge):

Spiritual Gifts and the Church
The Water That Divides
The Meal That Unites?
More Than Tongues Can Tell
Growing in God's Family

Contents

PART 5 • MARRIAGE AND DIVORCE

PART 6 • MARRIAGE AND THE FUTURE

Preface

LONG, long ago an infinitely wise poet declared:

> There are three things that are too amazing for me,
>   four that I do not understand:
> the way of an eagle in the sky,
>   the way of a snake on a rock,
> the way of a ship on the high seas,
>   and the way of a man with a maiden (Prov 30:18,19).

Who, then, am I to dare to write about that infinitely diverse, yet universally human relationship we call marriage? I married, 19 years ago, as England was about to beat West Germany at association football and win the World Cup. The game intruded into our wedding reception, as the guests gathered round a television, leaving us to depart for married life from an almost deserted railway station! Since then, we have lived in Sunderland and Derby and been blessed with three lively children.

During my marriage I have earned my living teaching Religious Education and Social Studies to boys and girls aged 11 and upwards in large, urban, multi-racial comprehensive schools. The impetus for this book came originally from the lessons I shared and the discussions I had with countless numbers of those young people. For all I have learned from them, I am deeply grateful.

I have also ministered in Baptist and Anglican churches and have found a particular interest in understanding the Bible's teaching on marriage, applying it to my own situation and proclaiming it to others. Since my ordination I have known the incomparable joy and privilege of preparing couples for marriage and presiding at their weddings. I have also known the heartache of sharing with others in their marriage difficulties, and sometimes in their breakdown. To all who have so kindly allowed me to share something of their experiences in the pages that follow I offer my sincere thanks. All their stories are essentially true, though their names have been changed along with some other salient facts, in order to preserve their anonymity.

This is not a book about how to be happily married: there are enough of these in print already. Nor does it give practical advice on marriage counselling. Rather, I examine the theology and ethic of marriage from, I hope, a biblical and Christian standpoint and with reference to particular issues as we face them at present. Nor is the final section, *Marriage and the Future*, intended to be comprehensive. Rather, I pick out one or two current initiatives by Christians which seem to me to point the way forward. Readers will know of others, and I hope they will be stimulated by what they read here, as well as by what they learn elsewhere, to give time, energy and prayer to preserving and protecting Christian marriage for the future.

Bible quotations, except where otherwise stated, are taken from the New International Version and are used with permission. Finally, my thanks are expressed to Rosalind Doig for her careful and painstaking help in proof-reading the text and compiling the Index.

Sunnyhill,
Derby, England.

July 1985.

Introduction

SHEILA was about twenty when she met and married George. Her parents were against the match from the start, aware of George's unstable character, and afraid the marriage would not work out. But Sheila was headstrong and madly in love, so she defied her parents and went ahead. Soon after the wedding George brought home a baby he had fathered by another girl, and Sheila agreed to mother the child as if he were her own.

Still George continued to chase the girls. For years Sheila never noticed. She was too busy caring for the adopted child, and bringing up two more of her own. But when the truth finally dawned she felt desperately rejected and alone. She suffered a total breakdown. For a whole year the children were placed in the care of the local authority, while she plumbed the depths of despair in the nearby psychiatric hospital. For months on end no man dared approach her, so violent was her rage on seeing him. When she was discharged from hospital and reunited with her children, Sheila tried a reconciliation with George. After a few brief weeks it failed.

Meanwhile, Tom and Marilyn were getting together. Their parents were against the match too, but, like Sheila and George, they went ahead regardless. They bought a home and furnished it. Two fine boys were born, and things were looking good. But problems with his parents from infancy had left Tom with a deep sense of inadequacy and an inability to relate to others. From time to time he passed through moods of black depression and violent, irrational behaviour. Disenchanted with the fickle nature of the man she had married, Marilyn turned to lovers for comfort and support. Soon, Tom and Marily were just another statistic among the ever-soaring numbers of the divorced.

In advanced societies around the world, Sheila and George, and Tom and Marilyn are increasingly typical of thousands of young couples who embark on the adventure of marriage and parenthood, yet whose hopes lie in ruins after less than ten years together. But they all shared something else in common besides their status as divorced people which, in theory at least, should have prevented their tragedies.

They all claimed to be Christians. From the outset of their marriage Tom and Marilyn attended their local church together. Even after Marilyn had left, Tom continued to take the boys to Sunday School, and to stay for the morning service himself. George said he was a Christian too, though it rarely showed! Sheila undoubtedly was, and no mere nominal Christian either. She rejoiced in a personal relationship with the living Christ. She knew the fullness of the Holy Spirit and exercised spiritual gifts in her private devotions and in the worshipping life of the church. Through all the trauma of her breakdown she never lost the sense of Christ's presence. She believed in her marriage and tried to make it work as long as she could, even when she finally realised she had made a dreadful mistake.

These two couples illustrate the growing problems we face as Christians. For years the steadily rising tide of divorce in society has broken against the rocks of Christian faith and practice, leaving the church relatively unscathed. 'The couple that prays together, stays together,' we said in our smug complacency. We turned a blind eye to the deep marital unhappiness which many Christians endured because they could not face the shame of admitting to failure. We quietly told the divorced they should not come to communion, and so we rejected and forgot them. The church was for nice people, happily married people, praying together people. It was not our business to pry into couples' personal affairs.

The last twenty years have changed all this. Fidelity and lifelong commitment have crumbled under the onslaught of the permissive society. Our congregations include more and more divorced people like Sheila and George, and Tom and Marilyn. More and more clergy are divorced too. Indeed, the Christian ministry is becoming a high risk profession in terms of marital breakdown. And as a new generation begins to turn to Christ from non-church backgrounds, so a growing number of converts are bringing tangled sexual and marital relationships with them into the life of the church. Their presence raises whole new questions of acceptance, forgiveness and discipline which, apart from missionary situations, we have never had to face before. If we do not tackle these issues urgently, anarchy will reign and our distinctive Christian witness will be lost. Already, in trendy churches in Boston, New York and San Francisco, large numbers of unmarried, sexually-active gays and straights are openly welcomed into their worshipping life.[1]

Because they were divorced and deserted, Sheila and Tom were desperately lonely. Each struggled to bring up their children on their own, while coping with the problems of maintenance and access

[1] Richard Holloway, *Responding to the Sexual Revolution, Church Times,* 30 July 1982.

which are the common lot of the single parent. For months they attended the same church, completely unaware of each other's existence and condition. But one Sunday morning they met over coffee after the service. Their common status gave them a natural sympathy for each other. Soon, they were deeply and genuinely in love. Words and natural fun flowed spontaneously between them. Their children were excited at the prospect of new parents. But when they said they wanted to marry they set a new problem. Could they do so, as divorced people, and remain obedient to Christ? Could they marry in church? If they went to the registry office, could they have a service of blessing afterwards and then continue in the life of the fellowship?

In the end, the minister married them. He exercised the right, which ministers in the Church of England have enjoyed since the Middle Ages, to marry anyone who is resident in the parish, as long as they are not married in law already. The law dissolved their first marriages.

Along with the leaders of the church, the minister reasoned that Christ could forgive their failure the first time round. Their marriages were dead. All hope of repair had gone. Tom's and Sheila's relationship with each other had not been a factor in the breakdown of their first marriages. They were determined to follow Christ together and to remain faithful to each other. Could not he, who makes all things new, heal the wounds of the past and unite them in a living demonstration of his undying love for his Church? If the vicar could ask Christ's blessing on a civil wedding, why not go the whole hog and give his blessing within the context of full Christian marriage?

So, with five children between them, Tom and Sheila again entered married life. At first, they enjoyed ecstatic bliss. Soon, yet another child was born to complete their joy. But they were always desperately short of money. Tom's modest wage was quite inadequate to meet the demands of a large and growing family. To make ends meet, Sheila returned to her work as a nurse, but she had to work at night while Tom was at home to look after the baby. Now that she had married again, Sheila's first husband George tried to withdraw the maintenance payments for his children; harrowing legal battles followed. Under the strain, Tom's periodic depressions returned, each time with increasing force and vehemence. Sheila's teenage children threatened to leave. After a particularly violent scene, Sheila herself left, taking all the children with her except the two boys from Tom's first marriage.

So what went wrong? Was the second marriage doomed from the start, the consequence of disobedience to God's law, because Tom and Sheila had remarried during the lifetime of their respective wife and husband? If so, where is divine forgiveness and the grace to begin again? Was the failure on a human level? Were the hurts, inadequacies and immaturities in Tom's and Sheila's characters such that they could never remain married to anybody? If so, what has happened to the sanctifying power of Christ who heals the brokenhearted and binds up their wounds?

Did Tom and Sheila marry too quickly? Was the presence of their children from their first marriages and their continuing dependence on George's maintenance payments, together with Marilyn's and George's access to their children, indications that the first marriages were not as dead as they thought they were? Should they therefore have waited, hard as it might have been, maintaining a mutually supportive relationship short of marriage until the children had grown up and left home?

Did the church fail Tom and Sheila? Some knew of Tom's earlier depressive attacks and kept quiet. Only one person advised caution, and her voice went unheard amid the general emotional excitement which accompanied the congregation's natural sympathy for two single parents who seemed, on the surface, so suited to each other. Did the church fail after they were married? Like many people they quarrelled about money and thereby added to their problems. Should they have been willing to accept more advice and supervision? If the minister had refused to marry them they would probably have gone to the registry office anyway, and what then?

Sheila is still a practising Christian. She has moved to another town and joined a lively church. Tom sits lonely and depressed at home, with his boys and his memories....

Widespread marriage breakdown throughout Western society has its roots deep in the past. Industralisation, urbanisation, the emergence of the nuclear family, the decline in family size, greater life expectancy, the rise of feminism and the demand for equality between the sexes have all played their part. But most insidiously, the impact of secular humanism as a philosophy of life has undermined the biblical and Christian principles on which marriage and society were based for hundreds of years. Christians themselves often come to marriage with the same secular presuppositions as their non-Christian contemporaries. They may be ignorant of the place of sex in marriage and may themselves be sexually experienced with others before they come together. They rarely take seriously the Bible's teaching on the relationship of husband and wife in marriage, and so they are surprised when the romantic love of their courtship disintegrates into quarrelling and strife.

Often they fail to use Christian principles in thinking about the place of children in their marriage, whether their problem lies in limiting the size of their family, or conversely in being able to have children at all. Mostly, they do not really understand what they are doing when they leave their parents and are joined to each other, nor why it is appropriate for the ceremony to be solemnised within the context of the church. Beyond a vague notion that God will bless them because they love him, even Christians are largely unaware of the divine dimension in their marriages; for them, like their contemporaries, marriage is a means to happiness and little more.

Christian leaders too are bewildered and confused with the problems of divorce, and the remarriage of divorcees, in the life of the church. Some take refuge in the certainties of the past, refusing to recognise divorce or to allow divorced people to remarry in any circumstances. Others, like the leaders already mentioned in Boston, New York and San Francisco, jump on the permissive bandwagon and lose their Christian identity. Most stumble from one situation to another, leaving confusion and hurt in their wake through their muddled thinking and inconsistent practice.

Western marriage is in crisis because we have abandoned the Christian principles on which our societies were founded and on which they grew strong. Christian marriage is in crisis because we have forgotten to obey the law of God and of Christ. In this, the Scriptures remain our guide, carefully understood and sensitively applied to the problems of our day. There are eternal principles which apply in every age and generation. There are difficult areas where changing conditions will demand careful and positive thinking. Sometimes, there are no easy answers. We live in a fallen world and we are all victims of our fallen condition. But the Christian way ennobles marriage, raises the status and dignity of women, provides a solid basis for family life and gives proper respect to children. It enables us to relate to the created order as God originally intended and so lays the foundation for true civilised living.

So this is a book on the theology of marriage, and on the ethical application of theology to the world in which we live. It does not give practical advice on how to be happily married, nor on how to help those with specific marital problems. Many other books are available in these fields and readers should refer to them for assistance. But I believe we shall not get our practice right until we start from a proper understanding of God's purpose in marriage from the beginning of creation.

Inevitably, I have written from a Western Protestant standpoint, for that is what I am. Primarily, I have written for other Western Christians like myself, faced with the moral confusion, wounded lives and marital breakdown of our contemporary scene. Of course, I recognise that different marital patterns exist in other cultures around the world. Nevertheless, I believe that in the Bible we can find proclaimed those eternal principles on which human relationships are meant to be built in all places at all times. The extent to which any society approximates to these will govern its overall health and integrity. The degree to which any man or woman obeys God's law will determine his or her ultimate eternal peace and security.

CHAPTER 1

In the Image of God

MARRIAGE began with God. It was established by him in the beginning when he 'created the heavens and the earth' (Gen 1:1). Any attempt to regard it as a purely human institution, invented by man to serve the needs of society, will distort our understanding. For if marriage is a human invention, different types of marriage have equal value. Polygamy, the taking of more than one wife, may serve one society; polyandry, sharing a wife between husbands, may serve another. Monogamy, the lifelong union of one man and one woman, has no more intrinsic value than any other kind of marriage. It simply emerges at a time in history when social conditions are suited to it, and it may be discarded when those conditions no longer exist. If serial monogamy, the taking of a succession of husbands and wives, comes to replace monogamy as society's norm, why worry? Monogamy has served its purpose; now let it be replaced by something else.

Male and female

As the crown of his creative activity, 'God created man in his own image, in the image of God he created him; male and female he created them' (Gen 1:27).

Both men and women enjoy an equality before him. Neither is superior to the other. In their relationship with each other, men have a primacy over women, which we shall explore in greater detail later, but in their relationship with God they are the same. They enjoy equal dignity and importance. He uses them both to achieve his purpose and will in the world. They come to him on exactly the same footing, through faith in Jesus Christ. As Paul says, 'there is neither ... male nor female, for you are all one in Christ Jesus' (Gal 3:28).

In these days of strident feminism, these truths are vital. Feminism represents an understandable reaction against the way women have been dominated by men, and against the way they have been undervalued by society for hundreds and thousands of years. Often, to their shame, Christians have accepted without question the attitudes of their contemporaries. But neither the Bible nor St Paul are anti-women, nor do they ever justify the degradation and exploitation of women which has characterised society in the past, and still continues in many forms today.

If God created man, male and female, in his own image, then it is wrong to think of God in a purely masculine way: for every masculine and feminine quality must find expression in his character. When we call God 'he,' and address him as, 'our Father,' we need to remember that we are using these masculine terms in a generic sense, as embracing the feminine as well. Many are protesting against sexism in our language and thinking at the present time. They claim that when we give a masculine gender to God we are implicitly debasing women. So we have attempts, for example, to rewrite the Lord's Prayer, beginning 'Our divine Parent,' and to retranslate the Bible removing all similarly sexist language. But if we remember that God made man male and female, and that we often use masculine terms to include the feminine as well, we should have no problems.

Be fruitful and increase in number

God is a creating God. Even though his initial work of creation is finished, he continues his creative activity. As long as the earth endures, seedtime and harvest, summer and winter never cease (see Gen 8:22). Within the created order God continues to create new life as plants, animals and humans reproduce and give birth. In the spiritual realm God is making everything new (see Rev 21:5). He brings new life to those who are dead in their transgressions and sins (see Eph 2:1). He tells us to be born again, of water and the Spirit, if we are to enter the kingdom of God (see John 3:3–5). He renews his church, forming its members into a living body and a holy temple.

So God gives to his created order a share in his creative work. Fish, birds and humans alike are specifically told to 'be fruitful and increase in number' (Gen 1:22,28), and the same command is implied to animals as well. To be sure, in Genesis 1 nothing particular is said about marriage, but a comparison with Genesis 2, and with other material later in the Bible, makes it clear that marriage is intended to be the relationship in which human reproduction takes place.

This divine command to be fruitful and increase in number is increasingly challenged and disregarded in Western society, even among Christians. The world population explosion, it is argued, has rendered it obsolete. Now we can best obey God and serve humanity, we are told, by limiting our reproductive capacity and even abstaining from it altogether. A growing number of people are coming to

7

marriage with the clear intention of avoiding children for the whole of their married lives.

Undoubtedly, population explosion is causing severe problems, notably in the third world. But the steadily declining birth-rate in Western Europe is also causing concern, as these now ageing societies are facing the prospect of caring for growing numbers of elderly people with a minority of productive workers.

God's command to be fruitful and increase in number comes at the beginning of the Bible's teaching on human relationships and marriage. It is not culturally conditioned, and is therefore integral to his design for humanity and the world. Nowhere in the Bible is it ever withdrawn, nor is there any suggestion that it ever will be while the present created order remains. Like all the rest of God's commands, we neglect it at our peril.

Rule over creation

Closely linked with the divine command to humanity to reproduce is the further command to rule over the created order. God blessed male and female and said to them, 'Be fruitful and increase in number; fill the earth and subdue it. Rule over the fish of the sea and the birds of the air and over every living creature that moves on the ground' (Gen 1:28). 'The Lord God took the man and put him in the Garden of Eden to work it and take care of it' (Gen 2:15).

This connection between mankind's creativity in reproduction and his sovereignty over creation is little appreciated and rarely explored, yet it is fundamental to our humanity as it reflects the nature of God. 'God said, "Let us make man in our image, in our likeness, and let them rule".... So God created man in his own image, ... male and female he created them' (Gen 1:26,27).

We are conscious today, perhaps as never before, of our need to relate positively to the world around us. If Christian marriage is in crisis, so is our rule over creation. Industrial processes are threatening global catastrophe through acid rain. Indiscriminate use of chemical fertilisers is destroying many species of animal and plant life. Destruction of tropical rain forests may be contributing to unforeseen changes in world climate. Mineral resources are being exhausted with little thought for the future. Over all hangs the threat of nuclear annihilation.

If marriage, as we have seen, is the proper relationship in which man may reproduce, might there not be a connection between the way we relate as husbands and wives and the way we exercise our sovereignty over creation? Could it perhaps be that our current disregard for our environment and our contemporary attitude to easy divorce, reflect our selfishness and greed? Will it not follow that when husbands exercise a proper headship over their wives (see Eph 5:23), instead of enslaving and degrading them, they will treat the world around them with similar concern and respect? We cannot separate our personal and our working lives. As we are in ourselves and in our closest human relationships, so we shall be in our attitude to the world God has placed in our charge.

A suitable helper

As the divine image is reflected in man's rule over creation, so it is displayed in the relationship of husband and wife. There is a plurality in the Godhead — 'Let *us* make man' (Gen 1:26). Although it is not currently fashionable amongst biblical scholars to see the Trinity anticipated here, developed Christian theology nonetheless understands God the Father, God the Son and God the Holy Spirit living in a union of eternal love. God intends men and women to display that same love in their marriage relationships with each other. 'It is not good,' says God, 'for the man to be alone. I will make a helper suitable for him' (Gen 2:18).

Significantly, in the twentieth century, this is what we want from marriage more than anything else. We no longer regard marriage primarily as a means of begetting children, or, through them, of providing security for our old age. Nor is it any longer a way to obtaining economic independence, a means of breaking free from the economic unit of our parents to form a new partnership of production. We marry because we want a satisfying relationship, one which fulfils our deepest needs and aspirations. This is God's aim for us too, which is why we find so much help in the Bible to enable us to achieve it.

So God forms a woman from one of the man's ribs (see Gen 2:21). Unlike the rest of creation and man himself, she is not made from 'the dust of the ground' (Gen 2:7), but from the man who will become her husband. She is called 'woman' because she is taken out of man. She is bone of his bones and flesh of his flesh (see Gen 2:23). From her, man himself will come as she and the man become interdependent on each other (see I Cor 11:11,12). Woman was 'not made out of … [man's] head to rule over him, nor out of his feet to be trampled upon by him, but out of his side to be equal with him, under his arm to be protected, and near his heart to be beloved.'[1]

One flesh

God makes a woman and brings her to the man. They are united and

[1] Matthew Henry, *An Exposition of the Old and New Testament*, comment on Gen 2:21–25.

9

become one flesh. They are both naked and feel no shame (see Gen 2:22,24,25). God is spirit (John 4:24), but the spiritual union of the Godhead is reflected in the physical union of husband and wife.

This union of man and woman in sexual intercourse is fundamental to marriage. Whenever Jesus and Paul discuss marriage they start with Genesis 2, and what they say follows from the Genesis principles. To be sure, the act of intercourse in itself, does not make a man and woman husband and wife, though it always affects them permanently, even in a fleeting relationship with a prostitute (see I Cor 6:16). But without intercourse, there can be no marriage.

Many years ago an unofficial story circulated about a prominent Christian and his wife. It was said that on their wedding night they had vowed to become eunuchs for the sake of the kingdom of heaven. In order to give themselves totally to the service of Christ they never had intercourse and thus avoided the distraction of bearing and raising a family. If the story is true, and we may be forgiven for doubting, then that man and woman were never fully married. Perhaps handicapped or very elderly people may marry without ever being physically united, but they are rare exceptions to a general rule.

Becoming one flesh implies continuity. We cannot become one flesh with a succession of husbands and wives as the modern practice of so-called serial monogamy implies. Only death can release us from the physical bond of marriage and free us to marry again (see Rom 7:1–3).

The one-flesh principle excludes polygamy and concubinage and all the other arrangements whereby men have tried to take more than one wife. We cannot become one with more than one other at a time. The Old Testament characters who took more than one wife found it caused them all kinds of problems. Their wives were jealous, or felt exploited, degraded or shamed.

Adultery is wrong because it attacks the marriage union. One party feels guilty, the other betrayed. Fornication is wrong because it antici-pates marriage. Are the couple married or not? No one is quite sure.

In married sex, men and women may feel no shame. The openly ero-tic language of the Song of Songs shows us that husbands and wives are intended to enjoy their sexual activity together. Some scholars believe that the Song may have been sung as the bridegroom led the bride in procession from her home to his to rejoice with their families and friends, and then to consummate their union together.

Paul says that in the marriage and physical union of a man and a woman lies a great mystery, which anticipates and reflects Christ's love for his Church (see Eph 5:32). Therefore we should have no fear in married love, for when we come together we are experiencing some-thing of the eternal union of the Godhead and the redemptive love of Christ for the world.

The way marriage is established at the very beginning of the Bible, in chapters which describe God's creation of the world, indicates its universality. God intends all women everywhere to be suitable helpers for their husbands. God desires men around the world to leave their fathers and mothers and be united to one wife. The existence of different marital patterns around the world only indicates the extent to which human relationships have been spoiled by man's rebellion against God. 'All have sinned and fall short of the glory of God' (Rom 3:23). Christian marriage ought not to be unique. Through their personal knowledge of God through Christ, and their obedience to his way, Christians should set a standard in marriage — God's standard — for the rest of mankind to follow.

CHAPTER 2

The Image Defiled

In the Garden where God had placed them, the man and woman sinned. Although he made every provision for their physical, emotional and spiritual satisfaction, they disobeyed him. They ate from the forbidden tree of the knowledge of good and evil. Mankind still suffers from their behaviour.

We need not be sidetracked with questions about the literal and historical nature of the Genesis story of the Garden of Eden. Its strongly symbolic language gives it an eternal quality which overrides such problems. It describes our condition now, just as much as it tells what happened to Adam and Eve. 'Sin entered the world through one man, and death through sin, and in this way death came to all men, because all sinned' (Rom 5:12).

In God's perfect creation, evil was already present. Its origin is a mystery. God is not its author, neither is it co-equal nor co-eternal with him. Yet God is a moral being. Every quality of goodness is expressed in his character. And if man is to reflect his image and likeness, he must be moral too. And he can only know goodness if he resists evil. In Hebrew thought, to know is to experience. God told the man and the woman to avoid experiencing what is good and what is evil. He had given them all they needed. He asked them to trust him, to avoid things they were not to know, to leave them alone.

But the man and the woman failed. They decided they knew best. Not satisfied with being made in God's image, they wanted to be as God himself, with all the totality of knowledge which is his alone (see Gen 3:5). They wanted to rule the world for themselves, not in trust from their Creator. They demanded to control its destiny in place of him.

The appeal of the tree of knowledge was physical (it was good for food), sensual (pleasing to the eye) and spiritual (desirable for gaining wisdom). Forbidden experience usually appeals to one or more of these three basic desires. It promises to satisfy physical needs of which we may feel unjustly deprived by an apparently kill-joy God. It sets our eyes on things rather than on God himself. And it promises enlightenment, despite the fact that God is light and in him is no darkness at all (see I John 1:5).

So the woman took some of the fruit of the forbidden tree and ate. She gave some to her husband, and he ate. The effects were immediate and dramatic. Their eyes were indeed opened, but the result was entirely the opposite to what they had expected. It is still the same when we eat forbidden fruit.

Broken relationships

As soon as they ate, the man and the woman 'realised that they were naked; so they sewed fig leaves together and made coverings for themselves' (Gen 3:7). Their lovely, unashamed relationship had gone. Not only did they hide their bodies from each other, but their true selves as well. They hid behind arrogance, self-righteousness and pride. Guilt and inadequacy ate at the heart of their being. Inner wounds and hurts destroyed their capacity to love and be loved.

When the man and the woman ate from the tree of knowledge, their relationship with God was broken. Not only did they hide from each other with fig leaves; they hid from God as well (see Gen 3:8). They still hide. They hide by denying him, by ignoring him and by distorting his image through false religion. No wonder marriage is in a mess. We have denied its divine dimension. We have made it a purely human affair, subject to changing social attitudes. We have left ourselves without a model or a pattern on which to make it strong.

Man's relationship with the created order was also broken. Not only the serpent, but all cattle and wild animals were cursed on his account ('cursed are you *above* all the livestock' — see Gen 3:14). The ground was cursed with thorns and thistles. Painful toil to win a living from it became man's unhappy lot (Gen 3:18,19). 'The whole creation has been groaning ... right up to the present time' (Rom 8:22).

Blame

With broken relationships came blame. "At last!" cried Adam when he first saw Eve (Gen 2:23 RSV). "At last! Bone of my bones and flesh of my flesh! Just what I've been waiting for! A suitable helper, at last!"

That joy changed to recrimination; "The woman you put here with me — she gave me some fruit from the tree and I ate it (Gen 3:12). It's all her fault! Don't blame me!"

How often the story is repeated! A boy and a girl fall in love. Neither can conceal the joy of their discovery of each other. She's the one! He's Mr Right! So they marry, raise a family, and over the years, unseen and unnoticed, here and there, little by little, communication breaks down between them, love grows cold. Their marriage ends in bitter recrimination. Each blames the other. Neither can see where they have gone wrong.

Pain

"'Be fruitful and increase in number,"" God had said; "fill the earth and subdue it"" (Gen 1:28). Husband's and wife's greatest joy, the bearing of children, becomes an experience of trouble, pain and sometimes death.

Nor is the pain restricted to pregnancy and giving birth. How many marriages begin to falter with the arrival of a family? 'Children make a marriage,' says the proverb. Often they break it. When children come, parents may quarrel over the way they should be brought up. Tiny children themselves can be difficult and demanding, taxing the most patient parent. Often wives lose their sexual desire after pregnancy, bringing new and unexpected strains to the relationship. In any event, small houses and wakeful children make lovemaking more difficult. A family can bring financial hardship and the evaporation of expectations.

When marriages fail, children are torn between father and mother. Bitter legal wrangles over custody and rights of access result in friction which can last for years. The children themselves may feel guilty and responsible for the breakdown of the marriage. Wounds are inflicted deep in their characters, which, in time, will make it all the more difficult for them to form stable and lasting marriages of their own.

Rule

Despite the pain of childbearing, the woman would still desire her husband and he would rule her (see Gen 3:16). God had made her to be a suitable helper; now she was to become a slave.

Man's subjugation of woman down the ages has been one of the greatest scandals of human history. He has exploited and degraded her. He has used her to gratify his desires and then has abandoned her. He has taken her as property, sometimes in great numbers, and through her has boasted of his wealth and power. He has beaten and abused her, within marriage and without. Yet still she desires him. Still she clings. Long-suffering wives still put men to shame.

Death

Saddest of all, through the sin of the man and the woman, death entered the world. "'You must not eat from the tree of the knowledge of good and evil, for when you eat of it you will surely die'" (Gen 2:17). And so they did. From the moment they covered themselves with fig leaves, they began to age. With ageing came weakness, the end of beauty, and in due time, death. Death spread to their offspring. 'Sin entered the world through one man and death through sin, and in this way death came to all men, because all sinned' (Rom 5:12). Our whole human personality was affected. Not only was there the prospect of physical death, but death towards God in our transgressions and sin (see Eph 2:1).

Death ends marriage. When a husband or wife dies the other is free to marry again (see Rom 7:1–2; I Cor 7:39). For, in death, the 'one flesh' relationship is finished. We shall certainly meet again in heaven, but not as husband and wife, for 'at the resurrection people will neither marry nor be given in marriage; they will be like the angels in heaven' (Matt 23:30). The original writers of the Book of Common Prayer understood this perfectly when they wrote in the marriage service, 'Till death us depart.' In Elizabethan English this meant, 'till death divides us into parts.'[1] Although always the widowed partner of the one who has died, the survivor becomes a separate person again, free to become one flesh with another.

Separation from a wife or husband through bereavement is one of the most painful experiences we may ever have to face, surpassed perhaps only by the death of a child. We feel lost, alone, bewildered and confused, adrift on an open sea. Part of us has gone, never to return. The death of a spouse brings home to us our sinful condition, whose only end is death for ourselves as well.

New hope

Nevertheless, the story of the Garden of Eden is not one of unrelieved gloom. In the heart of God's judgment lies promise, the first faint glimpse of God's mercy, the first indication that God will remake his broken world and restore the broken relationships which human rebellion have caused.

Despite the pain and the shame, the sweat and the toil, the curse and death, the offspring of the woman will crush the serpent's head, and he will strike their heel (see Gen 3:15). Mankind and Satan will be locked in enmity and struggle. Men and women will limp along, always striving yet always failing to become the beings they were intended to be. But eventually, the serpent will be destroyed. His head will be crushed. He will trouble us no more. And this will be achieved by the offspring of the woman herself!

Ever since the second century Christians have seen in these words the first distant promise of the coming of Jesus, 'born of a woman, born under law, to redeem those under law, that we might receive the full

---

[1] *Shorter Oxford English Dictionary, Depart.*

rights of sons' (Gal 4:4,5). Made sin for us (see II Cor 5:21), on the cross he was pierced for our transgressions and crushed for our iniquities (see Is 53:5). There Satan was dealt a mortal blow. His final end is assured. And through Christ's mighty resurrection a new humanity was born. New life was offered to all who believe.

To be sure, little of all this could have been in the mind of the original author of Genesis. But the Bible is a whole, not merely a collection of isolated parts, and we may rightly interpret its early statements in the full light of Christian revelation.

Because the divine image in man is defiled, Christian marriage is in crisis. When men and women marry without regard to God and then try to live selfishly together, lifelong faithful marriage falls apart. When Christians marry and do not live in obedience to God, the distinctive characteristics of Christian marriage begin to disappear, submerged by the secular attitudes of the world around them.

But in Christ, we can begin to be suitable helpers to each other, heirs together to the gracious gift of life (I Pet 3:7). No longer need we rule and be dominated: rather we can 'submit to one another out of reverence for Christ' (Eph 5:21). Once again, we can be naked and unashamed, physically, mentally and emotionally, because all our sins, our failures, wounds and hurts can be cleansed, healed and washed away. We can walk and talk with God in unbroken fellowship, as 'the blood of Jesus, his Son, purifies us from every sin' (I John 1:7). We can relate positively and constructively to the world around us, subduing the earth, ruling the animal kingdom, working and taking care of the land, given to us in trust from God himself.

CHAPTER 3

Love without Limits

God and his people

In God's eternal wisdom man's rebellion became the occasion for the revelation of the most wonderful aspect of God — his love. Already we have seen it foreshadowed in the Garden of Eden story, in the promise that the woman's offspring will crush the serpent's head. But in the Bible pages that follow love is shown more clearly in God's choice of Abraham to be the father of his people, and in his subsequent choice of the Israelites to demonstrate his love to the world.

Central to God's action is the idea of covenant. God chooses to enter into a solemn covenant of love with individuals, families, tribes and the nation of Israel. None of them deserves his love; it flows from his sovereign will and his free choice. Although he demands love in return, his love extends from generation to generation: his covenant is everlasting. 'The LORD your God is God; he is the faithful God, keeping his covenent of love to a thousand generations of those who love him and keep his commands' (Deut 7:7–9).

In God's covenant with his people the true nature of love is displayed: not as a romantic feeling which lasts as long as it receives love in return, but as a solemn decision, to be exercised whatever the cost, in faithfulness to a sworn promise. For God rarely receives the love he demands. Abraham, Isaac, Jacob and Joseph all disobey him to a greater or lesser degree. The Israelites are downright rebellious, constantly forsaking him for the worship of other gods. Still God goes on loving, and even though eventually Israel is all but destroyed, he still preserves a remnant through whom Christ is born.

Israel and the prophets

In the final dark days of the kingdoms of Israel and Judah, when the expansionist policies of neighbouring super-powers were threatening them with extinction, God made a series of final appeals to his way-ward, faithless people through a succession of prophets. Among these was Hosea, who declared God's love through the personal tragedy of his broken marriage and family life. God told Hosea to marry Gomer, a prostitute, and raise a family by her. When she went after her lovers, Hosea was sent to take her back to live faithfully with him for the rest of her life.

The message was clear. God was Israel's husband; Israel was God's wife:

> "In that day," declares the LORD,
> "you will call me 'my husband'; ...
> I will betroth you to me for ever;
> I will betroth you in righteousness and justice,
> in love and compassion.
> I will betroth you in faithfulness,
> and you will acknowledge the LORD" (Hos 2:16,19,20).

God's relationship with his people set a pattern for the relationship of husband and wife. Love, compassion and faithfulness, expressed in continuing forgiveness, lay at its heart.

A century later, Jeremiah's appeal was couched in similar terms. God had entered into a covenant with his people and become their hus-band (see Jer 31:32). Even though they had broken the covenant he remained faithful. In time he would make a new covenant. He would transform their hearts and make them his people for ever (see Jer 31:33). The parallel is clear. Marriage is a covenant, a solemn agree-ment made between a man and a woman to be husband and wife to each other until one of them dies. As God keeps his promises, they must keep theirs. Neither may break the agreement, whatever the other one does.

Jeremiah's message was ignored. Judah fell to the invading Babylo-nians. All her leading citizens were carried away into exile. There Ezekiel graphically declared God's unfailing love as a husband, wooing, winning and reclaiming an unfaithful wife. 'When I looked at you and saw that you were old enough for love ... I gave you my solemn oath and entered into a covenant with you ... and you became mine.... You adulterous wife! You prefer strangers to your own husband! ... I will sentence you to the punishment of women who commit adul-tery.... I will put a stop to your prostitution, and you will no longer pay your lovers.... Yet I will remember an everlasting covenant with you ... and you will know that I am the LORD' (Ezek 16 *passim*).

Isaiah similarly described the final restoration of Israel in terms of an ever-loving husband forgiving and restoring his errant and wayward wife:

"For your Maker is your husband....
The LORD will call you back
   as if you were a wife deserted and distressed in spirit —
a wife who married young,
   only to be rejected," says your God.
"For a brief moment I abandoned you,
   but with deep compassion I will bring you back"

(Is 54:5–7).

So the Old Testament prophets described God as the divine husband and Israel as his wife. God's love for his people set a standard for all husbands and wives to follow. Malachi, one of the last of the prophets before John the Baptist, made the practical application: 'The LORD is acting as witness between you and the wife of your youth, because you have broken faith with her, though she is your partner, the wife of your marriage covenant... "I hate divorce," says the LORD God of Israel' (Mal 2:14,16). Divorce destroys the one-flesh relationship of marriage, underwritten by God himself, for the purpose of raising godly offspring (see Mal 2:15). It is an affront to the nature of God who has shown husbands and wives how to behave towards each other through his faithfulness to his covenant with his people.

Christ and the Church

In Christ, all the hopes of the prophets find fulfilment. He is the one to whom they look forward. He is the mediator of the new covenant foreseen by Jeremiah, 'that those who are called may receive the promised eternal inheritance' (Heb 9:15). Significantly, the first act of his public ministry occurred at a wedding in the village of Cana in Galilee. There he was invited, along with his mother and his disciples as guests. During the week-long festivities, the wine ran out. Aware of the crisis, Mary told Jesus, "They have no more wine." Despite his initial reluctance to become involved, Jesus nevertheless told the servants to fill six stone jars with water and take some to the master of the banquet. As they did, the water was turned into wine. 'This, the first of his miraculous signs, Jesus performed in Cana of Galilee' (John 2:1–11).

Jesus' action was highly symbolic, involving far more than the mere provision of wine at a badly organised village wedding. The stone jars were there for ceremonial washing by the Jews (see John 2:6). They stood for the old covenant between God and his people, a covenant based on obedience to law, on perpetual sacrifice, on a mediating priesthood and on religious observance. When he turned the water into wine, Jesus began to show how he had come to cancel the written code with its regulations that are opposed to us. In due time he would nail it to the cross (see Col 2:14), thereby setting us free and establish-

19

ing the new covenant of the Kingdom of God. All the Gospel writers insist that the 'new wine' of this Kingdom cannot be contained in the 'old wineskins' of Jewish ritual and ceremonial law (see Mark 2:18–22).

In God's Kingdom, Jesus is the bridegroom; the people are the bride. When he was asked why his disciples did not fast like the disciples of John the Baptist and the disciples of the Pharisees, he replied, "How can the guests of the bridegroom fast while he is with them?" (Mark 2:19). Significantly, at Cana, the bridal pair are anonymous: the spotlight falls on Christ. By accepting the invitation and turning the water into wine, Jesus did far more than adorn with his presence the holy estate of Matrimony (*Book of Common Prayer*). He declared himself the true bridegroom. 'He thus revealed his glory, and his disciples put their faith in him' (John 2:11). 'Blessed are those who are invited to the wedding supper of the Lamb!' (Rev 19:9).

If Jesus is the bridegroom and those in the Kingdom of God are the bride, then Christ's relationship with his people sets the standard for Christian marriage. It is the natural development of God's relationship with Israel. Commenting on the Genesis statement that a man leaves his father and mother to be united with his wife and become one flesh with her, Paul says, 'This is a profound mystery — but I am talking about Christ and the Church' (Eph 5:31,32).

CHAPTER 4

Reflecting the Image

PENNY and Mike were set for a stormy marriage from the start. Penny was forceful, ambitious and demanding. Mike was shy and reserved. An unhappy childhood had left him subdued. Victorian attitudes had made him guilty about sex. After the ceremony they had difficulty in consummating the marriage. For years afterwards Mike was rarely able to satisfy Penny's insistent demands.

Penny's attitude, in turn, made things worse. Disappointment with Mike led to derision. Her disenchantment spread to every area of their married life. Overwhelmed by her demands and deeply ashamed of his failure as a man, Mike simply retreated into his shell. He refused to accept any real responsibility as a husband, or as a father to the children who somehow came along. Sadly, Penny could not keep her feelings to herself, nor even restrict them to a single confidante. Everybody in the little chapel to which they belonged knew about Mike's problems. Their constant quarrelling and her belittling of him in front of others was acutely embarrassing.

Like so many other young couples, Penny and Mike had entered marriage with little preparation for the problems that lay ahead, and with scant understanding of the Bible's teaching on the subject. They had a 'modern' view of marriage. The romantic love of their courtship would carry them through any of the storms that lay ahead. When, as students, they had occasionally read those parts of the New Testament letters which are addressed to married people, they had dismissed such ideas as old-fashioned and out-of-date. Paul hated women, did he not? And Peter, too, was a Jew, whose attitude to marriage was inevitably coloured by notions of male superiority and female subservience. How could men like that possibly have anything to say to people like Penny and Mike?

Undoubtedly, some of the teaching of the apostles is culturally conditioned and directed at specific situations which no longer apply. But when they talk about marriage, they always go back to the beginning, explaining and applying the universal teaching of Genesis in ways which rise above cultural and temporal differences.

Who's boss round here?

If, as we saw in the previous chapter, the union of a man and a woman in marriage reflects the union between Christ and his people, their relationship must reflect that also. 'The husband is the head of the wife as Christ is the head of the church' (Eph 5:23). Penny and Mike, and thousands of other modern couples, find this totally unpalatable. Here is Paul the Jew, Paul the misogynist, putting women in their place to preserve the *status quo*. Did not old ideas of ownership derive from such attitudes, the organisation of society to ensure that men continue to exercise power, that women serve them and are denied fulfilment and the free expression of their personalities?

To be sure, Paul's teaching has sometimes been abused. Some contemporary American writers, reacting against the excesses of the women's liberation movement, are using him again to justify their support for dominant husbands and subservient wives. But we should beware lest we dismiss him out of hand. For he constantly writes from eternal principles laid down in the beginning. 'A man ... is the image and glory of God; but the woman is the glory of man' (I Cor 11:7). 'Adam was formed first, then Eve' (I Tim 2:13). And everything he says is qualified by his basic advice, 'Submit to one another out of reverence for Christ' (Eph 5:21).

Is the husband, then, boss after all? Is his the right to work, while the wife's place remains at home? Is he to discipline the children, while she comforts them afterwards? Was Mike, shy and reserved, wrong to marry Penny at all, because she naturally 'wore the trousers' and wanted to direct the course of their marriage?

This is to take a fallen view of marriage. The woman was made to be the man's suitable helper. Only after they had sinned did God say 'he will rule over you' (Gen 3:16). The virtuous wife of Proverbs 31 is no meek stay-at-home, bearing her husband's children and darning his socks while he goes out to make a name fo himself. Rather, she is an active business-woman, dealing in property and merchandise. She has time for the poor and the relief of their needs. She enjoys an active teaching and counselling ministry, while her faith in God is the mainspring of her life. As a result,

> Her busband has full confidence in her
>   and lacks nothing of value ...
> Her husband is respected at the city gate,
>   where he takes his seat among the elders of the land.

Paul does not advocate a primacy of ownership, character and ability, but a primacy of love. 'The husband is the head of the wife as Christ is the head of the church.... Husbands, love your wives, just as Christ loved the church and gave himself up for her' (Eph 5:23,25).

Here is how I am to be the head of my wife; I am to love her with the love of Jesus. Jesus' love does not demand love in return, but gives and goes on giving even when that love is spurned. Jesus gave up everything for the church — equality with God, heaven's glory, eternal fellowship with the Father and the Holy Spirit, the right to an earthly home, to a steady job, to the understanding and acclaim of his fellows, to a fair trial and to a humane death. What am I willing to give up out of love for my wife?

Christ did not come to be served by the church but to serve (see Matth 20:28). Do I expect my wife to serve me, or do I give myself to serve her? Christ went to the cross for the church. Where will my love for my wife take me? Christ gave himself for the church 'to make her holy' (Eph 5:26), that is, to set her aside to belong only to him. Does my wife find it easy or difficult to remain faithful to me?

Christ's love for the church cleanses and improves. He washed her in his blood at the cross. Now he works by his Spirit 'to present her to himself as a radiant church, without stain or wrinkle or any other blemish, but holy and blameless' (Ephes 5:27). Jesus loves to make me and all his people like him. Does my love for my wife wash away her inner wounds and hurts and bring out the best in her character? Do I make it easy or difficult for Jesus to make her radiant and blameless? Jesus does not repress and inhibit my character but enables it to flower and realise its full potential. Is my wife suppressed or enriched through my relationship with her?

Christ constantly feeds and cares for his church — the present tense of the Greek verbs implies continuity (see Eph 5:29). His love never grows stale and old. Am I still finding new ways to show my wife how much I love her? Or did our love die some years ago? Because the church is Christ's body, he loves it as he loves himself. 'In this same way, husbands ought to love their wives as their own bodies' (Eph 5:28).

In this context Paul directs wives to 'submit to their husbands in everything' (Eph 5:24). He never suggests they should lose their identities. 'Wives, submit to your husbands,' he says, 'as to the Lord' (Eph 5:22). The boundless love of Jesus evokes a response of love from me: joyful, obedient love. And when I begin to love my wife as Christ loves the church, she should have little difficulty in responding to and submitting to my love.

The submissive wife is neither chattel nor slave, but a woman who is utterly loyal and faithful to her husband through thick and thin. She accepts his love, imperfect as it is, and loves unstintingly in return. As she loves, her true womanhood flowers and blossoms. She takes her place in the body of Christ, using the gifts the Holy Spirit has given her.

In that body there is neither male nor female, 'for you are all one in Christ Jesus' (Gal 3:28).

Penny's and Mike's problems were by no means unusual. Nor was there anything wrong with their differences in character. God had made them both the way they were, and he had brought them together in love. But when Mike shrank from accepting his responsibilities as a husband and a father, and refused to face the inadequacies in his character which made him such a disappointment, he failed to love Penny as Christ loved the Church. And when Penny in turn paraded Mike's faults before others, and publicly berated and humiliated him, she failed to submit to his admittedly imperfect love. She would always be the prominent partner. Together, forceful and reserved, they complemented each other. But when they fought and quarrelled, they failed to mirror the love between Christ and the church.

Today, Penny's and Mike's marriage has grown strong. Stern rebuke from a trusted pastor, deep repentance, prayerful counselling, the healing work of the Holy Spirit, and a new start far away from their original home have all played their part. As the inner hurts behind Penny's strident demands and Mike's guilt about sex have been healed, so their love has become mutually fulfilling; their three fine children are growing up strong in the faith of the Lord Jesus Christ.

Significantly, in his letter to the Ephesians, Paul's advice to husbands and wives follows hard on the heels of his command to go on being filled with the Spirit (see Eph 5:18). I cannot begin to love my wife as Christ loves the church unless I am filled with his Spirit. Nor can she submit to me as to the Lord except by the power of the same Spirit.

When we are filled with the Spirit our relationship with God is transformed and we are able to worship him in spirit and in truth (see John 4:24). If we are married, our relationship with each other finds fulfilment. The husband is able to love his wife as he loves himself, and the wife is able to respect her husband (see Eph 5:33).

Marriage 'in the Lord'

Most of the early Christians were either converted Jews, or Gentiles who had embraced, to varying degrees, the Jewish faith. Although they already believed in one God and aspired to high ethical standards in their personal lives, they were hardly ready for married life which reflected the love between Christ and the church. The oft-repeated prayer of the Jewish male, 'O God, I thank you I was not born a woman!' indicated his low regard for the female sex. He could divorce his wife 'for any and every reason' (Matt 19:3), although she had no freedom to divorce, further reflecting the deep inequalities which existed between men and women.

In Corinth and Ephesus, in particular, and doubtless in other places too, Christian converts also came from the openly pagan background which characterised large sections of society (see Acts 19:18,19; I Cor 6:9–11). How were such people, many of whom had lost all respect for each other through their openly immoral behaviour, to begin to aspire to the lofty demands of Ephesians 5?

First, Christians should marry only Christians. 'Do not be mismated with unbelievers,' says Paul (II Corinthians 6:14 RSV). His words may have a wider application than marriage, but they undoubtedly embrace it. Elsewhere, he counsels widows: 'she is free to marry anyone she wishes, but he must belong to the Lord' (I Cor 7:39).

On a purely practical level, this makes obvious sense; people's religious beliefs matter. If one partner in a marriage is a Christian and the other is not, there will be tensions which they can well do without. Whatever they might have agreed before they married about the freedom they will allow each other, practical problems will surface. On Sundays, one will want to worship while the other may wish to do something else. When children arrive, the Christian parent will teach them of Jesus, while the other may offer little encouragement and may actively try to turn them away from him.

Undoubtedly, some Christian and non-Christian partners enjoy satisfying marriages despite their differences, but many more face lifelong disappointment because their partner does not share their faith. They tread a tight-rope, attempting to be loyal to Christ and faithful to their wife or husband. For some Christians, a decision to marry only 'in the Lord' may become the supreme test of their obedience to Christ. Refusing the chance to marry someone they love because they do not share their faith will tear them apart. And because, in Western society, there are generally more Christian women than men, this agonising decision will mostly be faced by women, who as a result may remain single for the rest of their lives.

But Paul has more in mind than merely practical considerations when he tells the Corinthian Christians not to marry unbelievers. Really, he says, it is a contradiction in terms. A union between a Christian and a non-Christian is like a partnership between righteousness and wickedness, light and darkness, Christ and the Devil. There can be no agreement between the temple of God and the temples of idols. One is true and living; the others are a fiction and dead (see II Cor 6:14–16). So, whenever a Christian marries, for the first or any subsequent time, he or she should only marry someone who belongs to the Lord (see I Cor 7:39).

What then of those who disobey this command, or who are already married to an unbeliever when they themselves come to a living faith in Christ? Are they to dissolve their marriages, or not? Certainly not, say the apostles. Christians married to unbelievers should display the love of Christ in the same way as those with Christian partners themselves. 'Wives ... be submissive to your husbands,' says Peter, 'so that, if any of them do not believe the word they may be won over without talk by the behaviour of their wives.' Purity and reverence should characterise your lives. Beauty should spring from the inner self, 'the unfading beauty of a gentle and quiet spirit' (I Pet 3:1–6).

Paul says the same. 'How do you know, wife, whether you will save your husband? Or, how do you know, husband, whether you will save your wife?' (I Cor 7:16). Indeed, because of the one-flesh principle, the unbelieving partner is half way to salvation already. He or she is inevitably affected by his or her union with a Christian. God's grace is already directed towards them on account of their marriage. 'The unbelieving husband has been sanctified through his wife, and the unbelieving wife has been sanctified through her believing husband' (I Cor 7:14). This does not compromise God's love for everyone, nor does it ensure that unbelieving partners will automatically become Christians. But God's grace does flow in family channels. Just as the children of Christians are special to God, so are those whom they marry (see I Cor 7:14).

How faith in one partner affects the other will vary from couple to couple. Pat was a nominal Christian, attending church more out of habit than anything else. But when she moved to a new area, and started attending a different church, she soon came to a living faith in Christ. Six months later, her unbelieving husband said to her one day, "You know, looking at you used to be like looking at a black and white photograph. But since you became a Christian, it's like seeing you in glorious technicolour!"

Jane came to know Christ when she was engaged. Immediately, she was torn. Should she marry Brian, whom she loved deeply, or not? Against the advice of some Christian friends, she went ahead with the wedding, and began to pray that Brian, too, would be found by Christ. For several years she endured considerable hostility from her husband when she went to church, and when they discussed Christian things together. But, after the children were born, very occasionally at first, Brian began to accompany Jane on Sunday mornings. Slowly, as many prayed for his conversion, his attendance became more regular. Friendships were formed, and Brian was involved in the formation of a men's group. Then, during a service, he slipped quietly out of his place with Jane, and joined her at the communion rail. His 'sanctification' had borne fruit.

The outcome will not always be so happy. Derek had the beginnings of an alcohol problem when he and Dawn had to marry in their teens. Soon she was enduring a beating every Saturday after his night on the town. When Dawn came to Christ, her faith seemed to inflame Derek and make him worse. Although, for a while, Derek turned from drink and tried to follow Christ himself, in time he went back to it, and the beatings and the cursings against Christ and his church became worse than before. For her own protection and safety Dawn is having to separate from Derek. In such circumstances, says Paul, a believing man or woman is not bound, for God has called us to peace (see I Cor 7:15). Quite what Paul means by 'not bound' we shall discuss in greater detail later. Suffice to say, Dawn has done all she could to submit to Derek as to the Lord. Now the situation has become impossible she is justified in leaving.

Reflecting the divine image in marriage, displaying the love-relationship betwen Christ and his church, is one of the noblest callings that can come to a man and a woman. Lifelong loving fidelity does not come easily and naturally. But in Christ, and in the presence and power of his Holy Spirit transforming our inner lives, are all the resources we need to overcome our selfishness, and to resist every temptation, to remain true to him and to each other. In these days of casual relationships and easy divorce we need, more than ever before, Christian men and women who will determine to live obedient married lives whatever the cost, not covering up their imperfections for fear of social scandal and shame, but transformed by the renewing of their minds, to test and approve God's good, pleasing and perfect will (see Rom 12:2).

CHAPTER 5

The Sacrament of Marriage

The open secret

The union of a man and a woman as one flesh in marriage is a profound mystery, says Paul; and many would heartily agree! Then he adds, 'but I am talking about Christ and the Church' (Eph 5:32). He does not mean that marriage is mysterious. Rather, he uses the Greek work *musterion* in a technical sense to describe a truth long-hidden that has now been revealed.

Jesus is the focus of mystery. Through him, many truths about God that were long hidden from human understanding have now been displayed. God's eternal plan, 'to bring all things in heaven and on earth together under one head, even Christ,' is a mystery (Eph 1:9,10). For centuries, it was a close secret, known only within the eternal will of the Godhead. Now, through Christ, it is open for all to see.

God's determination to make the Gentiles heirs together with Israel, members together of one body, sharers together in Christ Jesus is another mystery that lies at the heart of the gospel. It 'was not made known to men in other generations as it has now been revealed by the Spirit to God's holy apostles and prophets' (Eph 3:1–6).

In the same way, Christ's love for his church is a mystery: a love which redeems his people and unites them to him in a living body, with himself as its head. For long it was hidden. Now it is revealed, and is seen most clearly in marriage. Marriage has always reflected God's eternal nature, and his covenanted love for his people. But now, Christ's redemptive love is seen in marriage as well.

Jack Dominian[1] has shown how marriage, at its best, has a redemptive effect on the partners. We all bring to marriage a mixture of good and bad experiences of love. Within the mutual trust of our relationship we disclose our psychological wounds to one another, and as we

[1] Jack Dominian, *Marriage, Faith and Love*, pp. 44,67,89.

accept and affirm one another in our weakness and hurt, we are healed. Dominian insists that the need for this process to occur, if we are to become whole and holy human beings, constitutes one of the strongest arguments for the permanency of marriage; for without the certainty of continuity, reliability and predictablity it cannot take place. It therefore follows that even in a marriage where God is not consciously recognised or honoured, Christ's redemptive love can still be seen.

From mystery to sacrament

As the fourth century drew to a close, the need for a reliable Bible became increasingly evident. Since the accession of Constantine in 313, the church had enjoyed unprecedented liberty and unparalleled growth. Helped by government protection and aid, buildings had sprouted throughout the Empire; converts had flocked to be baptized. Their demand for instruction in Christian living strained the church's resources to the limit. Latin was fast replacing Greek, the language of the New Testament, as the everyday language of the people. Yet Bibles in Latin were scarce and often unsatisfactory.

Jerome, one of the early church's most colourful characters and finest scholars, set himself to remedy the defect. In 382 he retired to a monastery in Bethlehem to devote the remaining 23 years of his life to the translation and exposition of the Bible into Latin. His resulting Vulgate (the Bible in the 'vulgar' or common tongue) became the church's 'authorised version' for the next 1,000 years. Modern scholars still consult it when making fresh translations today.

When Jerome came to Ephesians 5:32, 'this is a great mystery and I take it to mean Christ and the church,' he translated the Greek *musterion* with the Latin word *sacramentum*, from which the English 'sacrament' derives. At the time, *sacramentum* was the accepted translation of *musterion* and carried with it the idea of a hidden secret now revealed. Indeed, in late middle-English the word sacrament could still mean a mystery or something which had a secret meaning.[1]

But *sacramentum* also meant a sign, and this use of the word would grow while the idea of *musterion* would decline. Marriage, of course, is a sign as well as a mystery. It is a sign of God's eternal love in himself, of his grace in creation, of his faithfulness to his covenant with his people, and of his redemptive love in Christ. Used in this sense marriage is a sacrament and we need have no fear in so describing it.

[1] *The Shorter Oxford English Dictionary, Sacrament.*

Indissolubility

While Jerome was producing the Vulgate, Augustine, bishop of Hippo in North Africa, was also calling marriage a *sacramentum*. Brought up in a Christian home, Augustine had lapsed into paganism and immorality before being converted in Milan in 384. Thereafter he rapidly became one of the church's most gifted and profound thinkers. His influence on Christian thought has lasted to the present day; among Roman Catholics his teaching sometimes enjoys an authority equal to that of scripture itself.

When Augustine called marriage a *sacramentum* he meant it was a sacred sign of the unity between Christ and his church. Because Christ's love for his church never ends, neither can the marriage bond be broken. When a man and a woman promise to live together until death separates them, they are not merely accepting obligations to each other, but to Christ himself as well, to reflect in their marriage Christ's unbreakable love for his people. Therefore, divorce and remarriage could not be allowed, for they demonstrated failure, not merely between the partners and to honour their obligations towards each other, but also between the partners and Christ, to display his saving love in their lives.

As we shall see later, all the early Christian fathers had rejected divorce and remarriage on the basis of Jesus' teaching in the Gospels; out of obedience to Christ, marriage was indissoluble. But, by describing marriage as a *sacramentum*, Augustine gave a doctrinal strength to the idea of permanency in marriage which would continue to grow as the centuries passed.

Once it was accepted that marriage was *a* sacrament, the idea soon gained ground that marriage was one of *the* sacraments of the church, a sign of his grace, given by Christ himself, whereby he continues to show us his love. Baptism and the eucharist are the two principal sacraments, signifying the washing away of our sins and our redemption through Christ's death on the cross. During the Middle Ages, confession, penance, confirmation, marriage and ordination were added to the list. At the same time, the growing strength of the priesthood was giving clergy the exclusive power to dispense the sacraments in Christ's name.

During the twelfth and thirteenth centuries the notion of sacrament was developed by a group of Christians called the Schoolmen to make marriage, not merely a sign, but an effective sign of Christ's union with his Church. In other words, couples getting married do not simply promise to display Christ's love in their relationship together, but also receive from him the grace to do so. Marriage is now a sacrament in a technical sense: not just a sign, but also a means of grace. Divorce, from being not permissible, is now not possible. It is a contradiction in terms. Marriage, in essence, is indissoluble. Furthermore, if a sacrament can only be received at the hands of a priest, secular marriage or marriage by one not truly ordained is no marriage, for only in the priestly blessing is Christ's grace conveyed.

Scriptural support for this special sacramental view of marriage is often found in a particular interpretation of John's account of the wedding at Cana in Galilee. In Chapter three we saw how, at Cana, Jesus did far more than rescue the master of a badly organised Jewish wedding feast from acute embarrassment. By turning water into wine from jars normally used for Jewish rites of ceremonial washing, he vividly announced the coming of the Kingdom of God and declared himself as the true bridegroom. 'He thus revealed his glory and his disciples put their faith in him' (John 2:11).

Many Catholic Christians insist that at Cana, Jesus transformed marriage as well. From being a creation ordinance, established by God in the beginning for the whole human race, Jesus, it is argued, made marriage into a founding relationship of the Kingdom of God. No longer simply a reflection of divine love, Christian marriage becomes a visible demonstration of the kingdom of God at work in the world. Because Christ is the bridegroom and the church is the bride, Christians who marry are caught up into Christ's saving work and become partners with him in the calling of a holy people into covenant relationship with himself. Before Christ came, marriage was a 'secular reality': now it is a 'saving mystery.'[1] Because Christ's love for his Church never ends, and because, through the sacrament of marriage, all who receive it share in his saving love, the marriage bond can never be broken.

Great variety exists among Christians at large over the related issues of indissolubility and sacrament. Some believe marriage can be dissolved in certain circumstances. Others believe it is indissoluble out of obedience to Christ. Some believe it is a sacrament in the simple sense of sign, others in the more developed sense of a means of grace and a sacrament of the church. Some are indissolubilists but not sacramentarians, while others hold a strongly sacramental position yet allow dissolution and remarriage in certain circumstances. Many are confused, and much of the confusion stems from a lack of understanding of the meaning of sacrament, or from the fact that some use the word in one sense and some in another!

Problems with the sacramental position

A sacramental approach to marriage in its developed form is fundamental to the position of the Roman Catholic Church, and is shared by

---

[1] E. Schillebeeckx, *Marriage: Secular Reality and Saving Mystery, passim.*

many in other traditions as well. Undoubtedly, it is highly attractive. It stands in stark contrast to the moral confusion which is now so widespread in Western society. But is it right? Did Jesus really transform marriage when he changed water into wine at the wedding at Cana? Despite the weight of Catholic tradition, many Christians are doubtful. Some wonder if a sacramental view of marriage actually undermines it, and thus has the opposite effect to that which is intended.

For a start, it is difficult to find the teaching supported anywhere else in the ministry of Jesus. When he was asked about marriage, Jesus never suggested he was teaching anything new, but always went back to 'the beginning of creation,' basing his arguments and drawing his conclusions on the statements of Genesis 2 (see Matth 19:1–8; Mark 10:1–12). Of marriage, Jesus never said, "You have heard that it was said to the people long ago.... But I tell you" (cf. Matth 5:21,22,27,28,3l,32,33,34,38,39,43,44). Nor did Jesus ever say, "The kingdom of heaven is like a man and a woman who are married to each other." He did say, "'At the resurrection people will neither marry nor be given in marriage; they will be like the angels in heaven'" (Matth 22:30). If marriage is a founding relationship in the kingdom of heaven, is it not strange that in heaven itself it will have no place?

A Christian sacrament is an outward sign of an invisible grace, instituted by Christ himself and enjoined on his followers. Baptism and the eucharist are obviously sacraments for Jesus told us to practise and observe them. But he never instituted marriage. So advocates of the sacramental position have to say he transformed it. But Jesus never did that either, but always returned to eternal principles established in the beginning. Among the so-called 'seven sacraments' marriage sits most uneasily since it does not meet the criteria demanded of a sacrament.

A further problem with the sacramental position lies in the related issue of indissolubility. To be sure, as we have seen, one can hold the two positions separately, but in the Roman Church at least, each follows from the other. Marriage is indissoluble because it is a sacrament. Because it is indissoluble, that proves it is a sacrament. Tied up with this is the further problem of divorce, of which more later. But, marriage is not indissoluble. As we saw in chapter two, death dissolves marriage. Jesus himself is quite clear about this; 'when the dead rise, they will neither marry nor be given in marriage' (Mark 12:25). We shall not be reunited with our married partners in heaven, not as man and wife, anyway. We shall see them again, and we shall know as we are known, but death ends marriage. That is why we are free to marry again after a partner has died (see Rom 7:1–3; I Cor 7:39). If marriage is indissoluble, we are not free to marry again after we have been widowed. Within the Catholic tradition there has always been a tendency to draw this conclusion.

A third problem with a sacramental understanding lies in the distinction it draws between Christian and non-Christian marriage. Marriage is only a sacrament when it is undertaken 'in the Lord'. Otherwise it is merely a secular reality. But Jesus never draws such a distinction. He urges everyone to live as God intended from the beginning.

If marriage is only a sacrament when it is undertaken in the Lord, marriage between non-Christians is not therefore marriage in the truest sense of the word. Therefore, when unbelievers are converted we would expect them to want to reaffirm their vows in the conscious presence of Christ, that they might receive his sacramental grace. Surely, Jesus and the apostles would have demanded this if it were so necessary. In fact they never did. They never had any hesitation in urging Jews, who already stood in covenant relationship with God through circumcision, to enter into new covenant relationship with Christ through baptism. Whey then did they not demand remarriage from all their converts? Because there is no fundamental difference between Christian and non-Christian marriage. Marriage is a creation ordinance; it is not a sacrament in the technical Christian sense of the word.

Of course, when God has poured out his love into our hearts by the Holy Spirit (see Rom 5:5), we shall begin to love each other as husbands and wives as God always intended. But this is quite different from saying that marrige between the followers of Jesus possesses an essential quality which marriage between others does not have.

Further problems derive from the whole idea that in marriage Christians are somehow caught up into Christ's saving work in the world, becoming partners with him in the calling of a holy people into covenant relationship with him. Unless the nature of this partnership is very carefully defined it can compromise the totality and finality of Christ's work of redemption. In his life, his death, his resurreciton and ascension, Jesus did all that was necessary to bring us, and all creation, to the Father. He 'offered for all time one sacrifice for sins' (Heb 10:12). On the cross he cried, '"Finished!"' (John 19:30). His work was done. The work of salvation is his, and his alone.

To be sure, Christ continues to work in the world through his body, the church. He is its head. All who follow him are its members. He commands his church to make disciples of all nations, baptizing them and teaching them to obey him (see Matt 28:19). Through the church he continues to proclaim his saving love as he transforms and empowers its members by his Spirit. But salvation, redemption, transformation and the outpouring of new life are always his, and not ours. And they are always received through faith, rather than rites and ceremonies properly administered.

Within the totality of Christ's work in the church and in the world, married Christians undoubtedly have a vital role to play. Through their fidelity and the quality of their love for each other they proclaim

God's love for all to see. They set an example to the rest of society; this is how marriage should be, this is what God wants for you all. 'It is God's will ... that each of you should learn how to live with his own wife in a way that is holy and honourable, not in passionate lust like the heathen, who do not know God' (I Thess 4:4,5 margin). But unmarried Christians have a similar, equally valuable part to play. Through their chastity and self-control, they also proclaim God's saving power in their lives. They also tell the world how people should live. 'For God did not call us to be impure but to live a holy life' (I Thess 4:7).

In I Corinthians 7, Paul wrestles with the advantages and disadvantages of being married or unmarried for Christ's sake. 'An unmarried man is concerned about the Lord's affairs — how he can please the Lord. But a married man is concerned about the affairs of this world — how he can please his wife — and his interests are divided. An unmarried woman or virgin is concerned about the Lord's affairs: her aim is to be devoted to the Lord in both body and spirit. But a married woman is concerned about the affairs of the world — how she can please her husband.' Sadly, some have taken these words out of context to conclude that perpetual virginity is better than marriage. But Paul adds, 'I am saying this for your own good, not to restrict you, but that you may live in a right way in undivided devotion to the Lord' (I Cor 7:32–35). 'Each man has his own gift from God; one has this gift, another has that' (I Cor 7:7).

Paradoxically, those Christians who have strenuously held a sacramental view of marriage have often been those who, at a practical level, have eschewed it. In the Catholic tradition, marriage has been denied to priests and those who make religious vows. A negative approach to sexual activity, with the idea that original sin is transmitted through semen, has led many to conclude that the best Christians will avoid marriage. Celibacy is the ideal. Today, some Catholic writers, like Jack Dominian, are emphasising the value of marriage. Sacramental teaching in itself does not necessarily produce strong and healthy marriages. It can have the opposite effect. Indeed, at the practical level of day-to-day marital living, the sacramental position can create serious difficulties. It is one thing to say that the union of a man and a woman in marriage reflects the relationship between Christ and his church, for that gives us a standard to aim at. As a husband, am I really loving my wife as Jesus loves his people? As a wife, am I really submitting to my husband as to the Lord? But to tell a man and a woman that their marriage, by its very nature, proclaims the intimate love and response of Christ and his church, may destroy them, for if they are honest, they know that it rarely does this. Their love is imperfect. They quarrel. They fall short. Married people have enough problems to overcome, without being set an impossible standard they know they can never attain. Like the law which the early Jewish Christians wanted to impose on Gentile converts, it puts a yoke on their neck which they cannot bear (see Acts 15:10).

The trouble with the sacramental view of marriage lies in the way it is based on a speculative interpretation of a highly figurative passage of Scripture, the wedding at Cana in Galilee. This is not the way to establish Christian doctrine. Rather, we must look at the teaching of the whole of the Bible, particularly in its plain and easily understood parts, and understand the figurative passages in the light of these, instead of the other way round. When the Reformers did this in the sixteenth century they rejected the idea that marriage is a sacrament of the Church, established by Christ, as an effective means of grace. As a result, the status of marriage among Protestants was raised, and the way was paved for the emancipation of women and universal education. So the dignity of children was recognised as well.

If, when we describe marriage as a sacrament, we mean it is a sign of God's grace in creation, in covenant relationship and in redemption, we may use the term without fear. But if we use it in a technical sense to distinguish between Christian and non-Christian marriage, then we go beyond the teaching of Jesus and the apostles, with the consequent danger that our understanding and practice of marriage will become distorted and unbalanced.

CHAPTER 6

Contraception

MIDWAY through the third century, many aristocratic women in Rome were finding faith in Christ and joining the church. Convention, however, required that they should marry among their own social class, and Christian men of equal standing were in desperately short supply. Nevertheless, converts from lower strata were plentiful and were naturally attracted to these gracious Christian ladies. Marriages began to take place in which the partners understood, from the outset, that they would never bear children: had they done so the children would have inherited their fathers' social position and not their mothers'.

When Hippolytus, the bishop, discovered what was happening, he was scandalised. His protests began a tradition within the Christian church that persists to the present day: children are central to the purpose of marriage, therefore the use of contraceptive techniques constitutes disobedience to God's law. Augustine made this a cardinal doctrine of the church; it was eloquently and persuasively restated by Pope Paul VI as recently as 1968 in his encyclical, *Humanae Vitae*.

Contrary to popular opinion, contraception is not a Victorian invention, nor are contraceptive drugs a twentieth century discovery. The Romans had them in abundance, hence the 'unlawful' marriages against which Hippolytus thundered. Nor is contraception only a feature of developed societies: missionaries among Amazonian tribespeople have been offered leaves from various forest trees which are highly effective in preventing the arrival of children. Nor is contemporary Christian concern at the widespread practice of contraception the prerogative of the Roman Catholic Church: American evangelical writers Larry and Nordis Christenson urge Christians, even more eloquently than Pope Paul, to have large families, and to restrict their family planning to the rhythm method.

Whether we like it or not, contraception is fundamental to the pattern of Western marriage today. Couples generally delay the start of their families for about three to five years after getting married. They then space the arrival of subsequent children and limit their numbers dramatically. As a result, they can look forward to long years in middle life and old age when they are on their own, because their children have grown up and left home to start new families themselves. All this happens because contraceptive techniques are widely available and freely used. Christians, in general, follow the pattern of society around them, often unthinkingly. But should they? Does the Bible allow us to regulate the structure of our families in our own interest? Or does the command to be fruitful and increase in number mean we should leave the issue with God?

Are children fundamental to marriage?

First, [matrimony] ... was ordained for the procreation of children...
Secondly, it was ordained for a remedy against sin, and to avoid fornication...
Thirdly, it was ordained for the mutual society, help, and comfort that the one ought to have of the other, both in prosperity and adversity.

Marriage is given, that husband and wife may comfort and help each other, living faithfully together in need and in plenty, in sorrow and in joy. It is given, that with delight and tenderness they may know each other in love, and, through the joy of their bodily union, may strengthen the union of their hearts and lives. It is given, that they may have children and be blessed in caring for them and bringing them up in accordance with God's will, to his praise and glory.

The reversal of the order of the purposes of marriage in the introductions to the marriage services in the Book of Common Prayer and the Alternative Service Book 1980 reflects a revolution in Christian thinking which has taken place within the last hundred years. The Prayer Book restates the mediaeval position as established by the church fathers: marriage is primarily for the procreation and upbringing of children. Other considerations — control of sexual activity and love between husband and wife — follow from, but are subservient to this one main feature. In the twentieth century, we put relationship first, we talk positively rather than negatively about sex, while children take their place at the bottom, rather than the top, of the list.

This revolution in thought has come about through a change in our attitude to sex which, significantly, comes in the middle of both the Prayer Book's and the Alternative Service Book's definitions of marriage. According to Genesis, a man leaves his father and mother, is united to his wife, and they become one flesh (see Gen 2:24). The act of sexual intercourse makes them one (see I Cor 6:16). Even humanistic observers have noticed how sexual activity is generally more important to humans than it is to animals. The human female is almost alone among mammals in enjoying sexual orgasm as well as the male, and this, it is recognised, binds her to her partner emotionally as well as physically.[1]

Through sexual activity we also reproduce. The command, therefore, to be fruitful and increase in number, is a command to be sexual. When we obey it, and thereby become one flesh, we fulfil God's purpose for men and women. So sex in marriage has a twofold purpose. It both makes us one, and enables us to procreate. During the Middle Ages, Christians stressed the procreative aspect of sex while neglecting, and sometimes despising, its unitive purpose. Today, we stress its unitive role, and may ignore the command to be fruitful and increase in number.

Earlier in the book we argued that the modern position more accurately reflects the teaching of Scripture than the mediaeval. The woman was created because it was 'not good for the man to be alone' (Gen 2:18). But, through marriage and the birth of children, God has made men and women to reflect his image and to share in his creative activity. Therefore, generally speaking, marriage without the intention of children will fall short of God's purpose. The agonies through which some barren couples pass, and the lengths to which they go to have children, reflect this deep creative urge which God has put within us.

Of course, there will always be some exceptions to this general rule. Couples who are too old to have children may still properly marry. Those who know that one or both partners are infertile may also marry, as long as the issue of childlessness is squarely faced beforehand. Those who know they are carriers of genetic diseases may also decide they should avoid having children. But for the vast majority, marriage should embrace the intention and desire to bear children.

Modern contraceptive techniques have succeeded in separating sexual activity from childbearing. Married or unmarried, we may now enjoy a lifetime of sexual behaviour without ever having to consider that children may be born as a result. And evidence suggests that a growing number of people are taking the childless option when they

[1] See e.g. Desmond Morris, *Manwatching*, p. 250f.

decide to marry. They are not simply concerned to delay, to space and to limit the size of their families, but to avoid them altogether. Others delay their families for so long and, enjoying the high standard of living associated with two incomes and two careers, they also decide not to bother with a family after all.

To the extent that contraception makes this possible, I believe it can become dehumanising. We are not meant to separate sex from childbearing, and those who do, totally and finally, purely for personal reasons, are surely falling short of God's purpose for their lives. They run the risk that their marriage and sexual activity may become self-indulgent. They will only look inwards to their own self-satisfaction, rather than outwards to the creative experience of bringing new life into the world and nurturing it to maturity.

Sometimes, contraception extracts a high price. Often in a deliberately childless relationship, one partner discovers a growing desire for children. Then the other feels cheated. The initial agreement not to have children is threatened, and an unexpected strain comes into the marriage. Sometimes, sexual activity becomes revolting as its natural end product, procreation, is denied. Then the tension may become unbearable and breakdown follow. We are not meant to divorce sex from childbearing; if we try, we sometimes find we are unable to.

Contraception has also affected our approach to marriage. When people married with the firm expectation of becoming parents within a year of the wedding, I believe it made them far more careful about whom they were marrying. Declared love, without the desire for children, is often defective love. It is love which I want, rather than love I want to give. Anyone approaching marriage whose partner is reluctant to start a family, ever, should pause and reconsider their decision. Anyone who wants to marry and avoid children altogether should similarly pause, and ask themselves why. Are they so hurt by memories of their own childhood, or by strains in their parents' marriage, that they cannot face parenthood themselves? Is it right to commit someone else to marriage with the inbuilt contradiction of no children at its heart? Dare we enter marriage on our terms, rather than God's?

God commands us to be fruitful and increase in number. His words in Genesis, as we have already seen, are not culturally conditioned, but stand at the dawn of creation, his declared intention for the well-being of mankind. The population explosion has not rescinded them. World famine is more the result of human greed, exploitation, misuse of available resources and unwillingness to adopt more productive methods of agriculture, than the simple fact that there are too many people.

Once married couples have allowed themselves time to adjust to each other, I believe they should start their families as soon as reasonably possible, before they become accustomed to too high a standard of living which children might threaten. Of course, there might be pressing educational or financial reasons which may justify delay, but if everyone waited until they could afford to start a family, very few families would ever be started at all!

I believe we should be fruitful and increase in number. This is what God commands; that we replace ourselves and add to the human race. Since we need a birthrate of 2.1 children per woman just to maintain a stable population, this suggests aiming at families of at least three children. Again, there may be pressing medical reasons why some couples will properly settle for less, but I am suggesting a norm.

Western societies are currently ageing societies. Projections have suggested that at current levels of provision Britain will become unable to support its growing numbers of elderly people by the year 2020. The world as a whole may be facing a population explosion, but Western societies still need the vitality of youth if they are not to shrink and decline.

We may not need huge families any longer, but we still need families. Children need brothers and sisters if they are to grow into mature and whole adults, able to relate to others and to their wives and husbands in turn. Society needs Christian families, aware of God and his love through their own experience at home, and the teaching they have received from Christ's word.

Paul urges us not to conform any longer to the pattern of this world, but to be transformed by the renewing of our minds. Then we shall be able to test and approve God's good, pleasing and perfect will (see Rom 12:2). Because Western marriage has traditionally reflected Christian principles, many Christians in Western societies have largely felt justified in following contemporary trends as long as these did not compromise their fidelity to each other. But Western thought now increasingly reflects humanist principles, and this affects the way people marry and raise their families. We need to think and behave from Christian principles. If we marry, do we put the quality of our love for our partner before everything else: our careers, our social standing, the homes where we live, the cars we drive? Are we obeying God's command to be fruitful and increase in number, or do we put our own considerations, our own comfort, and even our service for Christ, first?

Children are fundamental to marriage. The whole nature of marriage and our sexual relationship says this is so. Christian ministers should therefore carefully question on this matter couples who are intending to marry, and point out the consequences if they refuse to obey God's will.

> Sons are a heritage from the LORD,
>   children a reward from him.

40

Like arrows in the hands of a warrior
  are sons born in one's youth.
Blessed is the man
  whose quiver is full of them (Ps 127:3–5).

Are children fundamental to sex?

If we may not generally marry without intending to bear and raise children, is it equally wrong to avoid conception during intercourse? Hippolytus gave a resounding affirmative to this question when he protested against the aristocratic Christian women of third century Rome. By the time of Ambrose and Augustine, in the fourth and fifth centuries, prohibition of contraception had become a cardinal doctrine of the church. At the same time, intercourse itself was becoming highly suspect, even for married people. Since semen was believed to be the means whereby our inherent sinful nature is transmitted from one generation to the next, sex for pleasure should always be avoided. 'Married people,' said Ambrose, 'must be ashamed whenever they think about the sort of life they lead.'[1] So marriage was only allowed as a 'medicine for lust,' and married people should only have intercourse when they specifically desired to bear children.

In the thirteenth century Thomas Aquinas reinforced this teaching by appeal to natural law. Since sex is so obviously connected with childbirth, intercourse was only not sinful if it was within marriage, if conception was desired and if it was not lustful. In the twentieth century Pope Paul VI has reaffirmed 'the inseparable connection, established by God, which man on his own initiative may not break, between the unitive significance and the procreative significance which are both inherent to the marriage act.'[2] In other words, sex makes two people one and is intended to produce children. We may not therefore be united sexually for one purpose and not the other.

Nor is this the exclusive position of Roman Catholics. Harry was a staunch Protestant Christian, firmly committed to membership of an evangelical 'holiness' church. He too believed that sexual intercourse was inseparably linked with the procreation of children. When he and his wife decided that they did not wish to add to the size of their family, Harry refrained from intercourse for the rest of his life, to his wife's great chagrin and disappointment. But is this position Scriptural? Are we to tell married Christians to avoid sexual union except when they want a child?

[1] Quoted in J. Rinzema, *The Sexual Revolution*, Eng. trans., Lewis Smedes, p. 59.
[2] *Humanae Vitae*, para. 12.

Sometimes, appeal has been made to the story of Onan in Genesis 38. He was younger brother to Er whose wife was Tamar. Because Er was wicked God slew him. By the Levirate law, Onan was then obliged to marry Tamar to produce offspring for his brother. But 'whenever he lay with his brother's wife he spilled his seed on the ground.... What he did was wicked in the LORD's sight; so he put him to death also' (Gen 38:9,10). However, a careful reading of the passage shows that Onan's wickedness lay not in his repeated acts of *coitus interruptus* but in his refusal to produce offspring for his brother, for he knew that 'the offspring would not be his.' Any children born to Tamar would legally have counted as Er's and, in due time, would have inherited his property. If Tamar remained childless, Er's property would remain in Onan's family.

The Bible, in fact, is silent on the subject of contraception. To be sure, sexual union makes two people one. It also enables them to conceive and bear children. But this does not necessarily mean they should only be united when they wish to have children.

We know, for example, that conception can only occur on two or three days of the woman's monthly cycle, and these cannot always be predicted with complete accuracy. Is intercourse at all other times, then, sinful? And what of the couple who learn that their marriage will always be infertile? Are they to refrain from all sexual activity as a result? Is sexual abstinence the only recourse for couples for whom further children would threaten the health, or even the life, of the mother?

Are couples who live to middle and old age to leave sexual enjoyment behind once they are too old to bear any more children? Will the act of marriage, which makes two people one, be sinful for those couples who marry when the wife is past the age of childbearing? The argument from natural law is, in fact, two-edged. Couples naturally have intercourse on many occasions when conception cannot take place. Is such intercourse unnatural, and therefore wrong? Within the overall relationship of marriage children should be desired, but not from every act of sexual union. Can there then be any fundamental reason why we should not purposefully avoid conception when we feel it is right to do so?

The ban on contraception, so fundamental to the Catholic tradition, fails to understand the effects of sin on marriage, sex and childbirth. Had we not sinned, we would not have needed contraception. Childbirth would have been easy and painless, and God's abundant provision would have more than satisfied our needs.

But sin has spoiled our world. The whole natural order has been affected by our rebellion against God. Thorns and thistles destroy our crops. The ground is cursed, and pests by the thousand eat what we labour so wearily to grow. Childbirth itself is particularly affected, a source of pain and trouble to millions of women the world over. Some women are fertile, able to bear twenty children within their childbearing years. Others are infertile, or can only conceive with difficulty.

Married couples in simple societies need large families, for half their children die at birth or in infancy. Those who survive will care for their parents in old age. But even in simple societies, some fertile couples come to the point where they can bear no more children. One more baby will push them over the margin between subsistence and starvation.

Large families in developed societies are not necessary; three or four children generally satisfy most couple's wishes. Since the State looks after the elderly, large families are not needed to share the load. In modern Britain the size of the average house alone makes large families an embarrassment. Because couples have higher expectations for their children than formerly, they are not willing to risk the mother's health with an endless succession of unplanned babies.

All these factors are the result of our general sinful condition. We are not all wicked, but we are all tainted by sin, and the societies in which we live are tainted too. Nor are Christians spared these general effects of sin. Christian mothers bear their children painfully, suffer from various gynaecological problems, enjoy different standards of living, and are faced with the same problems in their lives as non-Christians. Like any others, there may be all kinds of reasons why Christians may need to delay, to space and to limit the size of the families.

Humanae Vitae has, in fact, tempered the unyielding stance adopted by Augustine and Aquinas. Sexual union between husband and wife is no longer considered immoral unless directed to the procreation of children, but is 'honourable and good.' Nor does it cease to be legitimate when, for reasons independent of their will, it is foreseen to be infertile.[1] Therapeutic means may be employed to cure organic diseases, even though they have a contraceptive effect, and this is foreseen, as long as they are not used with a contraceptive motive.[2] In other words, a woman may take contraceptive pills to regularise her periods, so long as she still wishes to bear children. Whether or not she may take them if doctors consider it dangerous for her to conceive is not clear. 'Responsible parenthood' may also demand that a couple may choose to have no more children for the time being, or even for an indeterminate period.[3]

Nevertheless, according to the encyclical, artificial contraception remains unlawful. It is deemed to open the way to marital infidelity and immorality.[4] In fact, there seems to be little connection. Both vices

[1] *Humanae Vitae*, para. 11.
[2] *ibid.*, para. 15.
[3] *ibid.*, para. 10.
[4] *ibid.*, para. 17.

flourished in Victorian society, when it was alleged that the absence of contraception was a contributory cause: frustrated husbands, denied intercourse by their wives who feared more children, sought and found release with prostitutes. Contraception, says the encyclical, may cause a man to forget the reverence due to a woman, thus reducing her to a mere instrument for the satisfaction of his own desires, rather than a partner surrounded with care and affection.[1] Many husbands would doubtless argue that they use contraceptives because they revere their wives, because they care about their health and well-being, and because they want to show their affection for them, free from the anxiety of another unwanted pregnancy. Many wives would also want to insist that sex is not just something they do for their husband's pleasure, but something they enjoy too, yet they cannot if they are afraid of conceiving.

More persuasively, the encyclical argues that when contraception becomes an instrument of government policy for the control of population, it puts into the hands of public authorities the power to intervene in the most personal and intimate responsibility of husband and wife.[2] In this, it is absolutely right. It is as inhuman for any government to force contraception or sterilisation on anyone, as it was for Hitler to decree that all German women should give birth, irrespective of whether they were married or not, to strengthen the Aryan race.

In fact, like most other human inventions, contraception is morally neutral; it is what we do with it that counts. If we use it to practise sex outside marriage, or selfishly within marriage, or if through it we invade the privacy of others' marriages, we may indeed be guilty of disobeying the will of God and distorting the marriage relationship. But if we use it with a proper regard for the health and well-being of our partners and our families, then it can enhance and strengthen our marriages. Through contraception we can protect our marriages from the physical, emotional, economic and psychological strains they might suffer through further pregnancies, while at the same time we can use the act of marriage, reverently and lovingly, as it was intended, to bind us together in lasting union.

Read carefully, *Humanae Vitae* does say this. It is only in the means of contraception it prescribes that it is at its most controversial and, I believe, disappointing.

Are some contraceptives lawful for Christians, and others not?

This is the nub of the position adopted by *Humanae Vitae*: abortion, sterilisation and all forms of artificial contraception should be avoided, but Christians may restrict their intercourse to infertile periods in the

[1] *Humanae Vitae*, para. 17.
[2] *ibid.*, para. 17.

wife's menstrual cycle if they wish to avoid having children. Human beings 'are not free to act as they choose in the service of transmitting life, nor are they free to decide for themselves what is the right course to follow.'[1] But the rhythm method, as it is commonly called, is 'a facility provided ... by nature,'[2] and may therefore properly be used to limit and space the arrival of children. 'To experience the gift of married love while respecting the laws of conception is to acknowledge that one is not the master of the sources of life but rather the minister of the design established by the Creator.'[3]

Here is powerful stuff indeed, which should not be lightly dismissed by Christians, whether they are Roman Catholics or not. Artificial contraception does have drawbacks, and Christians like others can fall into the trap of using it selfishly. Barrier contraceptives remove the spontaneity from lovemaking and are messy to use. The coil may increase the pain and the flow of the menstrual period. Some regard it as an abortive rather than a contraceptive and are doubtful about the morality of using it as a result. Drugs can have unpleasant side-effects in the short run, can affect a woman's desire for intercourse, and can produce longer-term medical complications. Sterilisation suffers from an awful finality which some individuals and couples may later regret. Men sometimes feel they have lost something and have problems with impotence as a result.

Like the rhythm method itself, none of the artificial contraceptives is completely safe in its ability to prevent the birth of unwanted children. In addition to unreliability, artificial methods can cause side effects, which do not occur with the rhythm method. It also constantly keeps the childbearing aspect of lovemaking before a couple, even if they feel fully justified in avoiding children. Undoubtedly, some people find it an excellent contraceptive. 'When we got married,' said Frank, 'I bought a little dial thing from the chemist. I set it every month on the day my wife started her period, and it told me the days on which we should avoid intercourse. It worked perfectly. We had two children when we wanted them, then one day my wife said, "I think I'm pregnant again!" She was too! One of our children had found the dial in my bedside drawer and reset it!'

Nevertheless, a deep contradiction lies at the heart of Pope Paul's encyclical. Surely, in the eyes of God, it is the thoughts and intentions of our hearts that count, rather than our obedience to legalistic rules and regulations. This is the whole force of Christ's teaching in the Sermon on the Mount. What is the essential difference between a couple avoiding children for a lifetime by restricting their lovemaking to the

[1] *Humanae Vitae*, para. 10.
[2] *ibid.*, para. 16.
[3] *ibid.*, para. 13.

wife's infertile periods, and another couple avoiding children with the pill and sterilisation? Both, surely, are refusing to face up to their responsibility to 'be fruitful and increase in number.'

Nor does the encyclical's distinction between natural and unnatural methods of contraception withstand close scrutiny. Are the hormones in contraceptive tablets natural or unnatural ingredients? Is an Amazonian tribeswoman who eats certain leaves to avoid bearing more children behaving naturally or unnaturally? What is unnatural about using rubber to form a barrier to prevent conception? Have we used our minds naturally or unnaturally to find technological solutions to the problem of unwanted pregnancies? We are constantly using unnatural means to affect the natural functions of our bodies. Remember the well-meaning Christian opposition to the development of anaesthetics a hundred years ago? Is it natural or unnatural to remove cancer surgically, or to destroy it with lasers?

Sadly, for all its apparent theological and ethical precision, *Humanae Vitae* leaves much to be desired. Much more positive and challenging, I feel, is Larry and Nordis Christenson's approach in *The Christian Couple*. They advocate the rhythm method of family planning on the grounds that it enhances a couple's relationship. After twelve years of marriage they grew disenchanted with other contraceptive methods, not because they failed and brought unexpected children into the family, but because Nordis came to 'detest the sense of intrusion they brought into our relationship.'[1] Their first attempt with the rhythm method resulted in pregnancy, because they had miscalculated, but the baby miscarried. Thereafter, with growing confidence, they discovered the method was as effective and reliable as the others they had tried, with none of their psychological drawbacks. Furthermore, 'our sexual relationship developed in a new way. We love and delight in each other more. Sexuality has become a more enjoyable, natural part of my life. We attribute this to our discovery of natural family planning.'[2]

Nordis' chapter, *Contraception: Blessing or Blight?* deserves to be read and digested for its critique of our contraceptive mentality alone, and the harmful effects this has on human relationships. She rightly insists on the importance of children in Christian marriage, and on the value of self-control. During her fertile period a husband can show his love for his wife in other ways, then, when they come together, their joy is all the sweeter. 'A courtship and a honeymoon every month,' is how one couple described their experience with natural contraception.[3]

[1] Larry and Nordis Christenson, *The Christian Couple,* p. 73.
[2] *ibid.,* p. 75.
[3] *ibid.,* p. 86.

Nordis argues her case with sensitivity and restraint. The rhythm method is 'a viable option which merits serious consideration.'[2] Other, equally godly women, and men, would agree, yet would reach a different conclusion. Having tried the method themselves they would insist that the constant calculation of days, regular temperature-taking and observation of vaginal discharges constitutes as much of an intrusion into their marriages as Larry and Nordis found barrier and chemical contraceptives. Having accepted their family responsibilities, they have also found that the prospect of further conception and parenthood into old age has seriously inhibited their sexual relationship.

In our case, after joyfully wanting and welcoming three children into our family, we both came to the point where we knew that, whatever may happen to any of us, neither of us will want to become a parent again. It then seemed right to proceed with sterilisation. We have never regretted our decision. Our sexual relationship has been enhanced as a result. Freed from the need to prepare for sex, and from fear at the prospect of another child, we have been able to make love spontaneously, giving ourselves totally to each other in commitment and joy.

With the possible exception of the coil, which may be an abortive rather than a contraceptive, I can find nothing intrinsically wrong with any of the contraceptive methods currently in use in Western societies. I think the pill will come under increasing scrutiny, but this will be for medical rather than moral reasons. A 'morning-after' pill will clearly be an abortive and will raise moral issues on this ground alone; already it is being prescribed as an emergency measure, though it is not available for routine use.

More serious is our general contraceptive mentality whereby we are increasingly separating the unitive and procreative aspects of sexual behaviour from each other. In so doing we are causing enormous moral damage to ourselves and to our children, many of whom are growing up with little sense of right and wrong where sexual activity is concerned.

We have no right, as Christians, to avoid having children altogether when we marry and make love. But we have a duty, before God, to become responsible parents, giving our children warmth, love and focussed attention, bringing them up 'in the training and instruction of the Lord' (Eph 6:4). How we do this will vary from couple to couple, as we prayerfully seek God's will in the timing of our children's births, and the means we employ to this end.

[1] Christenson, *op. cit.*, p. 86.
[2] *ibid.*, p. 76.

CHAPTER 7

Infertility

BETWEEN seven and ten per cent of married couples are infertile.[1] Finding a safe and satisfactory contraceptive is not their problem. And the desire for a child can be overwhelming, threatening the most stable and enduring marriage. Some couples, it seems, will go to almost any lengths to obtain a child. They will pay huge sums of money, devise complicated legal formulae, and undergo prolonged, advanced medical treatment, all to have a child or children they can call theirs.

In society at large, and among Christians in particular, childless couples rarely find compassion and understanding. The popular myth that there is 'something wrong' with one or both partners dies hard, and finds expression in television situation-comedy jokes. At the same time, the contemporary church's preoccupation with the family, as expressed in family services, family holidays, family counselling, infant baptismal and dedication celebrations can leave a childless couple feeling lonely and isolated. What have they done to deserve such a fate?

Infertility in the Bible

Interestingly, the Bible has more to say about childlessness than about our modern problem of too many children. When Jacob's wives, Leah and Rachel, vied with each other to bear children for their husband, God was always at the centre of the action. 'When the LORD saw that Leah was not loved, he opened her womb, but Rachel was barren.' So Reuben was named, 'Because the LORD has seen my misery,' and Simeon, 'because the LORD heard that I am not loved.' After the birth of Judah, Leah cried, 'This time I will praise the LORD.'

When Rachel complained about her sister's fertility and demanded children of Jacob, he retorted angrily, 'Am I in the place of God, who has kept you from having children?' Eventually, 'God remembered Rachel, he listened to her and opened her womb' (see Gen 29:31—

---

[1] D. Gareth Jones, *Brave New People,* p. 94.

30:24). In the same way, the Lord closed Hannah's womb, and then in due time, remembered her and gave her a son (see I Sam 1:1–20).

Ascribing childlessness to God did not, however, prevent Old Testament characters from trying to do something about it. Frequently they prayed, and sometimes, as with Leah, Rachel and Hannah, God answered their prayers. Indeed, a constant theme runs through the Bible describing God intervening in apparently hopeless situations, not merely to satisfy barren couples' desire for a child, but, through the child who was born, to demonstrate his grace and saving power to his people. Isaac, Jacob, Joseph, Samuel, Samson and John the Baptist were all born to parents as desperate as their modern counterparts at their infertility. All of them, in some way, demonstrated God's use of his power, sometimes apparently overriding natural laws of conception, in order to keep his promises. Finally, through Jesus, conceived in Mary's womb while she was a virgin, God brought hope and salvation to mankind (see Matt 1:18–23; Luke 1:26–38).

God does hear childless couples' prayers, and they should never cease to pray to him. He may not always answer in the way they expect or would naturally desire, but he always hears. Like Hannah, they may have to examine their motives before receiving a reply (see I Sam 1:9–11). Like Manoah and his wife, who gave birth to Samson, their longed-for child may cause them great sacrifice and much heartache. It could not have been easy letting Samson's hair grow and denying wine and unclean food. His rebellion against their authority, his embarrassing encounters with the Philistines and the tragedy of his final end must have broken their hearts, but through it all God was at work on behalf of his people. Others may always be denied a child of their own, but may nevertheless find their parental instincts and gifts fulfilled in other, quite surprising ways.

Old Testament characters, however, did not stop at prayer. In addition, they employed other, biological and legal means, to circumvent the problem of infertility. While these were acceptable in the cultural climate of their day, they were not always satisfactory. From them, I suggest, we can glean principles which we can apply to our own, very different situation, and thus avoid making some of their mistakes.

Throughout Old Testament times, and into the intertestamental and New Testament periods, the Levirate law applied when a husband died, leaving his wife childless. Then, his brother or another close relative was required to marry her. The first son born of the union counted legally as the heir of the deceased husband (Deut 25:5,6). He perpetuated his name and inherited his property. Thus, a child born naturally of one father counted legally as another's.

Some Levirate marriages worked. Boaz' and Ruth's is the most obvious example; David and Jesus were both descended from that. But, on the whole, they do not seem to have been either popular or successful. Onan's behaviour towards Tamar, wife of his brother Er, provoked God's judgement. Later, Judah's failure to give the next brother to his daughter-in-law, Tamar, resulted in an incestuous affair (see Gen 38). Relatives were so reluctant to marry childless widows that they had to be threatened with public shame to make them comply (see Deut 25:7–10).

The Levirate law was designed to keep a man's property within his family. Nevertheless, by bringing in a substitute father it seemed to upset the delicate nature of the marriage relationship. Often, of course, the Levirate husband was married already, and took his brother's widow as a second wife. Even though that was socially acceptable, it nevertheless produced its own problems, and provided a further intrusion into another marriage relationship.

The Levirate law applied when a childless husband died. For the barren wife whose husband lived, social custom provided another way out of the dilemma. She simply gave one of her slaves to her husband and then claimed legal parenthood over any children who were born as a result; in this case a child born of one woman counted legally as another's.

Abraham and Sarah resorted to this practice when Sarah gave Hagar to Abraham and Ishmael was born as a result. The subsequent strife and tension it brought into their home and family life must have made them both rue the day they doubted God's promise to give them a child of their own (see Gen 21:1–21). Jacob's experience was no happier. His children born to Bilhah and Zilpah only increased the jealousy of his wives whose slaves they were. Again, intrusion by a third party and the children of a third party into an existing marriage relationship, produced great tension and caused great harm.

Like our Old Testament counterparts we too are faced with the problem of how far we may go in using natural and legal means to overcome infertility. Sometimes, a solution is deceptively easy. A doctor friend of mine has discovered that, for many couples, the rhythm method in reverse is all that is needed. 'Work out your fertile days,' he advises couples who consult him. 'Avoid intercourse, and any other form of release, for a week beforehand. Then enjoy yourselves!' Time and again, such simple advice is all that is needed. The moral integrity of the marriage is in no way threatened, and the agony of childlessness rapidly becomes a thing of the past. Nor can there be any inherent moral objection to the use of fertility drugs, even if septuplets are born as a result! But are we perhaps in danger, with some of our other solutions, of intruding into marriage to an unacceptable degree, with possible unforeseen consequences to the couples and the children who are involved?

Adoption

Michelle was nearly 17, eighth in a family of ten. Small in stature, all her life she fought for recognition from her parents and elder brothers in the large and noisy family where she seemed so insignificant. One night, she was gripped by fierce pains. She was in labour, although neither she nor anyone else had realised she was pregnant. Before dawn, she gave birth to a beautiful baby girl. Her father cursed her, and placed the child for adoption. Michelle was bereft and lost; her most precious possession had been taken away.

Ruby and Albert found Leila, Michelle's child, through the Catholic adoption agency with whom she had been placed. In their mid-thirties, they had always longed for a child of their own, yet all their efforts and the best treatment that medical science could offer had failed. In the end, they settled for adoption, and Leila seemed just right. Yet even as they signed the papers and went to collect her, Ruby was seized with guilt at taking another woman's child. That guilt would cloud her relationship with her adopted daughter for the next twenty-three years.

Michelle, meanwhile, was finding a growing affection for Paul. He had known her when Leila was born, though he was not the father. By the time Michelle was nineteen she and Paul had married, a gloriously happy marriage with both of them enjoying a growing faith in Christ. Perhaps because they had known the agony of separation and rejection they began to foster children with the encouragement and support of the Social Services department of the local authority. And eventually they adopted one of these children, once it became clear his natural parents would never want him again. They also had three fine children of their own. But they never forgot Leila. Although they knew they must never try to see her again, they prayed for her, and celebrated her birthday every year.

Years passed. Leila grew from childhood into teens, a bright, intelligent girl, the image of her natural mother in looks and determined personality. Teenage rebellion widened into a deep rift with her adoptive mother, though as yet she was unaware of the true nature of the relationship. Only when she left home for university, began to sleep with Phil, found she was expecting his child and decided to marry him, did Ruby tell her who she really was. Immediately, she longed to trace and meet her natural mother. But would her mother want to meet her? Would she want to know her after twenty years of separation?

Fearful of rejection, Leila held back for four years. Meanwhile, something deep inside was telling Michelle that Leila was in trouble and longing to restore the natural relationship broken at birth. When Leila's letter finally landed on her doormat Michelle was hardly surprised.

But the tracing of natural parents does not always result in a happy ending. Michelle's and Leila's reunion has brought back all the trauma of Leila's birth with the bitterness and resentment it created between Michelle and her family. Harsh words have flown between Leila and Ruby as the pent-up resentment and guilt of a lifetime have been expressed.

Wisely, Michelle rang the adoption agency through which Leila had been placed with her new parents. Was there, she asked, anyone who had experienced reunion, who could talk to her and guide her for the future? They told her that hundreds of reunions are now taking place every year, but they could only quote one instance nationwide where it was felt a truly happy relationship had followed. So many adopted children are experiencing secondary rejection by their natural parents that the agency is now advising them not to trace.

At the moment, things are looking good for Leila and her natural and adoptive parents. Michelle and Ruby have corresponded and are now planning to meet. If anyone can make it work, Michelle can. Her husband and Leila's are completely supportive. Michelle's other children are overjoyed at finding their long lost sister, and at discovering they are already aunt and uncles! But Michelle's adopted child now wants to find his real parents too...

Adoption has long been regarded as the easiest and most obvious solution to the twin problems of infertility and homeless children. Recognised and regulated by law, all parties were protected, it was thought, from exploitation, intrusion and possible revenge. As long as there was a ready supply of babies for adoptive parents the system seemed to work well. Disinterested and compassionate agencies, usually with a Christian foundation, ensured that babies were placed in secure, loving homes where the new parents were given advice on adapting to their new role. Occasionally magazine articles explored some of the less satisfactory effects of adoption, but on the whole society and childless couples were well pleased.

Now, however, as Michelle's and Leila's story shows, we are increasingly realising that adoption is not without its deep and lasting problems. Of course, it often works. Children settle happily with adoptive parents, grow to maturity and, in time, form strong marriages and settled families of their own. But they also suffer a crisis of identity, not only when they learn their true position, but for years afterwards. Now that they have the right to know about their natural parents, they sometimes resent their legal parents and question their motives. Nor are the adoptive parents themselves necessarily free from feelings of guilt, as Ruby found, however honourable their desire for a child in the first place. They rarely seem able to forget that he or she is adopted.

'I'm increasingly advising couples against adoption,' says a vicar of 30 years' experience. 'It creates such enormous problems of identity.

Fostering, yes! That's fine, but not adoption!' Fostering is a genuine act of compassion, providing an unwanted child with a home. It involves no deception, nor does it lay any obligations on the child. Contact with the natural parents can be encouraged and maintained, while the whole relationship is usually supervised by a professionally trained third party. Fostering is by no means ideal and can go horribly wrong with deep distress to all involved. On the other hand, with adoption we bring a child from one union into permanent relationship with another. In this way we interfere with the delicate and unique relationship which exists between husband, wife and their offspring and, in so doing, it seems we may cause long-term problems of which we may be quite unaware. Some will disagree with this controversial conclusion, but others are equally willing to reconsider the issue in the light of modern knowledge.

Artificial insemination

Adoption is a purely legal arrangement: the child of one union becomes the child of another with all the rights and privileges that follow. Other ways round the infertility problem may be recognised in law, but involve a different route.

Through contraception we separate sex from conception. Modern medical technology can now separate conception from sex, and is increasingly doing so to help infertile couples have a child. One tried and tested method is artificial insemination. Sperm from a husband is implanted into his wife's womb when she is most likely to conceive. Often it is successful and no moral objection need be raised. The child belongs to his parents just as if he had been conceived naturally. If we accept that we may use artificial means to prevent conception, there can be no essential difference between using them to enable it.

When, however, artificial insemination by husband (AIH for short) fails after three attempts, many doctors suggest using donor sperm instead. Sperm from an anonymous and unknown source is injected into the womb and conception may follow. Both husband and wife usually have to agree to artificial insemination by donor (AID), but whose is the child? It may be the wife's but it is certainly not the husband's. In English law it is illegitimate, but not in some American states.[1]

The intention may be different, but the parallel with Levirate marriage is obvious. A substitute father is used to provide a child for another man. Some Christians have tried to argue that AID is tantamount to adultery, because the result is the same as if a wife conceives during an affair. But this can hardly be the case, since, unlike Levirate marriage, no physical contact occurs between the wife and the

[1] D. Gareth Jones, *Brave New People*, p. 96.

donor; indeed, she does not know who he is!

Nevertheless, genetic material from outside the marriage is used to produce a child, and this can threaten even the most stable of marriages. The total effect is likely to be quite unforeseen when a couple agree to the technique, and may cause lasting harm to them and the children who are born by this method.

As we have already seen, adopted children like Leila long to know their real parents and sometimes go to extreme lengths to trace. Their right to know is now recognised, but the same right is denied to AID children. Even their parents do not know the identity of the natural father. Will not this create even greater problems of identity than it does with adopted children, if and when they discover the true nature of their parentage? Can we be certain that deep unease will not develop within the heart of the growing child regarding his relationship with his mother's husband, thus sowing the seeds of emotional problems?

Mothers like Michelle, who are separated from their illegimate children, never forget. Neither do fathers, though they are usually ignored. Might it not also be true that men who donate their sperm for artificial insemination discover a longing to know where their children are? Ensuring they can never know will not solve their problem.

AID is widespread; 10,000 injections are made in the United Kingdom alone each year. In the United States, 300,000 children have been born through the process.[1] Because of the anonymity involved, half brothers and sisters must run the risk of inadvertently marrying each other in due course.

Medical students and other hospital residents of comparably high intelligence are often used as donors. In America in 1979 they were being paid up to $35 for each ejaculation.[2] Sperm can be frozen and stored in banks for use when needed. Some banks are about to start direct marketing to the public. The secrecy which surrounds AID is designed to protect donors and doctors rather than the recipients and their children.

Because sperm from healthy young men are used for artificial insemination, children born by this method suffer less from genetic defects and other inherited disorders than children who are born naturally. Most doctors who offer AID are concerned to do no more than produce healthy children for their patients. But the Repository for Germinal Choice in San Marcos, California, has gone further. There the donors are Nobel prizewinners in science and other similarly high achievers. The recipients, too, must be healthy young women, under thirty-five years of age and of superior intellect. Although total

---

[1] D. Gareth Jones, *Brave New People*, p. 95.
[2] *ibid.*, p. 96.

anonymity is maintained, intending parents may choose sperm from donors with known characteristics. The aim, apparently, is to breed a new generation of creative scientists who, in turn, will benefit mankind.[1] But dreams of breeding a super-race are as old as man himself. They fail to take account of human sinfulness, and always end in ruins. They represent an attempt to re-erect the Tower of Babel (see Gen 11:1–9), to usurp God's position of sovereignty over his universe. Like the builders of old, God confuses their language and their plans come to nothing.

In vitro fertilisation[2]

If artificial insemination fails, couples may now be offered *in vitro* fertilisation (IVF). The birth of Louise Brown by this method in Oldham, England, in July 1978, was hailed as a medical breakthrough. Others have followed around the world. Eggs from a mother are fertilised by sperm from the father in laboratory conditions. One of them is then placed back in the mother's womb where, it is hoped, it will implant and grow to full-term and birth. Again, as with artificial insemination, if the sperm and egg come from husband and wife, and if the fertilised egg develops within the womb of its natural mother, there can be no essential moral objection. However, aspects of the technique and variations in its application are causing growing concern among Christians and non-Christians alike, and are likely to be the subject of debate for some years to come.

Sometimes, for example, a mother's egg and a donor's sperm may be fertilised before being placed in the womb. Conversely, a father's sperm and a donor's egg may be fertilised and then implanted in the wife. Or the fertilised egg of a husband and wife may be placed in the womb of a surrogate mother, who carries and bears the child before returning it to its parents. Parellels with AID and with the Old Testament practice of slave-mothers can easily be seen here, and open the whole process to the kind or reservations we have already discussed. Surrogate motherhood, or womb-leasing as it is sometimes called, is proving particularly controversial, not only because the idea of one woman bearing a child for another is repugnant to some, but also because the mothers involved are commanding increasingly high fees for their services.

IVF is only one application of the emerging and fast-developing science of embryology, in which research is being carried out on fertilised ova in attempts to determine the source of genetic disease. Inevitably,

[1] D. Gareth Jones, *Brave New People*, p. 97.
[2] For a fuller discussion of the issues raised by IVF see ibid., chapter 5, the Warnock Report, and the Church of England report, *Personal Origins*.

this means that fertilised ova then have to be destroyed when experiments on them are complete. Do these ova possess the attributes of human life? May we then use them and discard them in this way, however laudable our motives?

Current opinion is deeply divided. The recently published Warnock Report has recommended licensing of all laboratories engaged in embryonic research, and restriction of research to the first fourteen days following fertilisation. The British Government has promised legislation in due course. Meanwhile, a private member's bill, sponsored by Enoch Powell, to ban research on fertilised ova altogether has failed to win support in Parliament. The Church of England report, *Personal Origins,* compromises by suggesting that research is only permissible for seeking to resolve the problems of infertility and genetic disorder. For other goals it is not acceptable.

Clearly, we are at the beginning of a revolution in scientific capability and understanding which could increasingly separate human reproduction from sexual activity. This is unlikely to happen on any large scale; nevertheless, as Christians we shall require vigilance and constructive thinking if we are to protect the sanctity of human life as made in the image of God for future generations.

CHAPTER 8

Betrothal and Pledge

KINSHIP and marriage patterns around the world, particularly in tribal societies, are wide and varied. Their study is a favourite occupation among many anthropologists.[1] The great differences that exist serve as a salutary reminder that our own pattern is by no means the only one. Nor is it necessarily based on, nor even derived from, obedience to the law of God. Like most marriage patterns, it represents a response to economic and religious circumstances, and as these change, so does the nature of marriage. In some simple hunting and food-gathering societies, husbands and wives live faithfully together out of necessity, in order to survive and raise their families. Other circumstances favour polygamy or polyandry. Talk to any missionary about the difficulty of establishing monogamy in the latter environment! This does not nullify God's law, nor does it justify departure from it. But it does remind us how human sin and greed has spoiled, not only our individual lives, but the whole of society and our social organisation as well.

Edmund Schillebeeckx has traced the origin of marital practice in the West to a time in Roman society when every family worshipped its own household gods, the symbols of its ancestors. The head of each household was also its priest; to him was entrusted the care of the gods. Before he died, he passed on this care to his eldest son, who passed it to his son in turn and so on. Marriage therefore was essential, to ensure continuity of the family line and worship of the family gods; from the beginning it was an act of deeply religious significance.[2]

Inevitably, in the distant past, marriage was more often an agreement between fathers than between bride and groom. Because she was

---

[1] See, for example, Robin Fox, *Kinship and Marriage, An Anthropological Perspective,* for a useful introduction to the subject.
[2] E. Schillebeeckx, *Marriage: Secular Reality and Saving Mystery,* Vol. 2, p. 3f.

capable of bearing children, and thus ensuring the continuation of another family's religious tradition, a marriageable girl was a valuable economic asset. Nevertheless, whenever marriages were arranged, the right of the partners themselves to agree to the match was recognised. Without this consent, freely given, there could be no true marriage. When Abraham's servant, Eliezer, travelled to Mesopotamia to find a wife for Isaac, Rebekah had to be asked, 'Will you go with this man?'" (Gen 24:58). Without this agreement the marriage would have been void.

When a couple agreed to marry they were betrothed. Betrothal, unlike modern engagement, was binding; it marked the first stage of marriage. A pledge, usually a ring, was given to the bride by the groom, and although the couple continued to live apart, they became husband and wife. Thus Mary, who was 'betrothed' to Joseph was also described as his 'wife' (Matt 1:18,20, RSV).

Betrothal, as a separate act prior to marriage itself, establishing the legal bond between husband and wife, survived into the sixteenth century. Thus, for example, Martin Luther was publicly betrothed to Katherine von Bora on 13 June 1525, but did not marry her until 27 June.[1] However, by the Middle Ages, clandestine marriage was rife. Women were particularly at risk and were often forced into betrothal against their will. In isolated village communities, marriage between close relatives was widespread too. In England, to stamp out abuse, betrothal was made completely public and incorporated into the beginning of the whole marriage ceremony. When the priest says to the bridegroom, 'Will you take this woman to be your wife?', when he similarly addresses the bride, and when each replies, 'I will,' they are in fact making a legal response and becoming betrothed. The remainder of the ceremony is the marriage celebration proper, in which the bride is given to her husband, the couple make their vows to each other, and seek God's blessing on their union.

When betrothal and marriage were brought together, intention to marry was achieved through the publication of banns. From the Old Teutonic *bannan*, meaning 'to proclaim under penalty,'[2] the names of those planning to marry were called on three successive Sundays in their parish churches. Any who know of any 'just cause or impediment' to the marriage were required to declare it.

But betrothal would not die, and resurfaced in the modern custom of engagement. There is something particularly appropriate in a couple agreeing to marry before they actually do so, and in making public proclamation of their intention. They need to give their consent to each other privately, and then before others. They need a final period of preparation before they enter into life as husband and wife together.

[1] Roland Bainton, *Here I stand*, p. 289.
[2] *Shorter Oxford English Dictionary, Ban.*

Consent to marry is freely acknowledged and openly encouraged in modern Western society. At a formal level, parents have very little to do with whom their children marry, though their unseen influence may be considerable. But some couples misunderstand what they are actually doing when they agree to become husband and wife. Because they agree to marry they believe they can agree to separate. More and more are giving their consent in the traditional form while making the mental reservation that they can always have a divorce if things fail to work out.

Marriage has become inextricably linked with romantic love. We marry because we fall in love. If we fall out of love, then we imagine we should fall out of marriage. Since romantic love, at least in its initial form, rarely lasts indefinitely, more of us are taking the second action as well as the first.

We do not understand very well that the act of consent is an act of the will. '*Will you* take this woman to be your wife? *Will you* love her, comfort her, honour and protect her ...?' And the bridegroom answers, '*I will.*' Love may be sparked by emotion, linked with and producing feelings of tender affection, but love is a decision, supported by the will. *I will* love my wife, *I will* forsake all others, *I will* be faithful to her as long as we both shall live, irrespective of how I feel. I will love her when I feel like loving her, and I will love her when I do not feel lovingly disposed to her. I will love her when she loves me, and I will continue to love her when her behaviour does not evoke nor deserve my loving response.

Nor do we understand that marriage is a lifelong relationship, whether we like it or not. We cannot marry, and then become unmarried as if we had never married. Once we marry, we are permanently affected. If we divorce, we come as married people to any second or subsequent marriage. In Western society we have become so obsessed with ideas of romantic love and human happiness that, in false pursuit of them, we allow people to make the most solemn, lifelong promises to each other, and then to break them with hardly any penalty. Consequently, the promises are becoming increasingly meaningless and a growing number of people are despising them altogether.

People who live in societies where marriages are arranged between parents understand much more clearly than we do that love is consequent on marriage rather than a prerequisite for it. This is not an argument for arranged marriages, but a recognition that our understanding of the nature of love may be defective. When Paul commanded husbands to love their wives as Christ loved the church, he understood that love was a decision and not a feeling. No feelings of romantic love could have taken Jesus to the cross, yet he went because he loved us. In the same way we are to love each other, whether we like it or not, and in so doing, to fulfil our consent to each other, to be husbands and wives together as long as we both shall live.

CHAPTER 9

Leaving and Cleaving[1]

AT the end of the betrothal period, the bridegroom in ancient Roman society gathered his family and friends together and went to the home of the bride's father. There, in solemn ceremony, the bride was formally handed over to her husband. Then, the bridegroom led her, in joyous procession, to his own home. She was often veiled and dressed in white, and accompanied by her own family and friends. Singers and dancers escorted the bridal pair, neighbours and passers-by paused to watch, flowers were thrown along with good luck charms and the like. Sometimes, as in Jesus' parable of the wise and foolish virgins, it was late at night before the procession finally reached the bridegroom's home (see Matt 25:1–13).

There, the bridegroom solemnly lifted the bride over the threshold, and the guests followed them inside to a feast. During the feast, wedding-cake was eaten as a very holy pledge of the marriage that was taking place. Often, the feasting went on for several days; at Samson's wedding it lasted a week (see Judges 14). Sometimes, as at Cana in Galilee, the wine ran out before the end (see John 2). When the feast was over the bride and groom retired to a special room to consummate the marriage. On the following day, the bride in ancient Rome made suitable offerings to the household gods whom she would now worship. The bridegroom presented her with a 'morning gift.'

Throughout antiquity, with minor variations, this pattern of marriage was more or less universal from India to Europe.[2] Readers will recognise how, in form at least, much of it has survived to the present day. The church or registry office may have taken the place of the bride's home, and a hotel may be used for the feast. Modern rapid

---

[1] For an outstandingly positive and practical application of this area of married life to contemporary American society, and, by implication, to the rest of Western society, see John and Paula Sandford, *The Transformation of the Inner Man,* ch. 19.
[2] See E. Schillebeeckx, *Marriage: Secular Reality and Saving Mystery,* Vol. 2, pp. 3–6.

transport systems have produced the honeymoon, with consummation also taking place away from the home, but otherwise the pattern remains intact. Limousines to and from church; the veil, the dress and the bouquet of flowers; the giving away of the bride and the ring; the feast and the cake — all have their origin in a distant past totally different from today's urbanised, secularised, computerised society. Yet the survival of these traditions is evidence of the unchanging character of human nature, and the continuing importance of marriage.

The way we marry reflects the biblical principle that, 'a man will leave his father and mother and be united to his wife' (Gen 2:24). In fact, because mankind is sinful, our marriage patterns only reflect the Bible's teaching imperfectly. Failure to understand what is involved in 'leaving and cleaving' lies at the heart of marital breakdown.

Significantly, only the bride is given away, though the Bible says, '*a man* will leave his father and mother.' What was intended to be a change in relationship became a transfer of ownership. Girls belonged to their fathers until they belonged to their husbands. At one time, no self-respecting father would agree to his daughter's marriage unless he was suitably compensated. The higher his social position the greater the bride-price. Equally, an intending bridegroom expected his bride to come suitably equipped to be his wife: the accumulation of money and possessions she brought with her constituted her dowry. Bride-price and dowry are combined today in the gifts which both families give to the bride and groom at their wedding.

Not surprisingly, in today's world of emancipated women, many have reacted against the whole concept of ownership in personal and marital affairs. Women do not belong to their fathers and husbands as if they were part of their property. If daughters should be given away, why not sons as well? The Church of England has responded to these pressures by making the giving away of the bride optional in the Marriage Service in the Alternative Service Book. Most couples still request it however; old habits die hard!

Leaving

If we are to marry successfully we must both, husbands and wives, leave our parents. In some societies, only the wife leaves, and she then goes to live with her husband's parents! In other societies, the opposite occurs. In today's Western society where the nuclear family is normal, many couples still find difficulty in leaving their parents. Their marriages suffer, and sometimes break down, as a result. 'My first marriage would have survived,' said a colleague, 'if it had not been for my wife's parents.' They had a home of their own, but she had failed to leave in the fullest sense of the word, and tragedy followed.

Leaving our parents when we marry does not mean we never see them again. Nor does it mean we evade our responsibility towards them as they grow old. Jesus scorned the hypocrisy of the Pharisees because they encouraged adult children to give to Temple funds the money they had set aside for their parents' old age (see Mark 7:9–13). Paul warned, 'if anyone does not provide for his relatives, and especially for his immediate family, he has denied the faith and is worse than an unbeliever' (I Tim 5:8).

When we leave our parents we leave behind our position as dependent children. Even when we have come of age, if we still live at home we remain dependent on our parents to some degree. On marriage, therefore, we should set up home together. Housing problems and social customs sometimes make this difficult, but as long as we live in the home of a parent we shall find it difficult to adjust to married life, and to grow together as married people.

This is not an argument for the nuclear family, husband, wife and children living apart from other members of their families. We do not have to move far from our parents' homes. We do not have to cease social contact with our parents and other relatives, but as married people we need to live on our own.

We need to end financial dependence on our parents. The couple who never learn to stand on their own feet financially will have little chance of becoming suitable companions for each other. Similarly, we must leave behind their authority. Interfering parents who are possessive, and who expect their married children to continue to do as they have always done, will threaten the best marriage. Their efforts should be stoutly resisted.

When we marry we may need to leave behind some of our parents' attitudes and influence. We may find this difficult, since we become the people we are largely because of the way we have been brought up. There will be conflict in every marriage as two different people learn to live happily together. In the process of give and take we need to distinguish between what was fundamental and what was peripheral in our upbringing, and to leave behind the latter for the health and growth of our marriage.

Most important, and perhaps most difficult of all, leaving our parents demands that we leave behind the inner wounds and hurts we bring to our marriage from childhood. Jack Dominian has shown how, in any marriage, we ultimately use all the emotional experiences we learned in the first two decades of our lives. We come to each other with a mixture of good and bad experiences of love. As, in love, we open ourselves, our bad experiences are healed and left behind. We forgive our parents for their failure. We grow to maturity in mutual trust.[1]

[1] Jack Dominian, *Marriage, Faith and Love,* pp. 34,35,44,67.

In today's society, more and more people seem to be coming to marriage with such deep wounds and hurts from their childhood that they are unable to relate to each other with the depth which is necessary for their healing. Yet we also live at a time when the Christian church is rediscovering its healing ministry. Through a living relationship with Christ himself, and the healing power of the Holy Spirit, we can be delivered from the wounds that bind us. Filled with the love of Jesus we can be set free, and so express the suitable help God has always intended we should give to each other.

Cleaving

As we leave our parents, we must cleave or be united to each other. The close relationship we once enjoyed with our parents is transferred to our partner. We become dependent on each other. The well-being of our spouse should become the priority of our lives.

In the older translations of the Bible, the word cleave denotes warm togetherness and support in every experience of life. The word is used when Ruth refused to leave her mother-in-law Naomi, but determined to remain loyal to her and accompany her home to Bethlehem. Orpah, at Naomi's behest, returned home, but Ruth 'clave unto her' (Ruth 1:14 AV). Similarly, when Absalom rebelled gainst his father, King David, the men of Israel united behind him, but the men of Judah 'clave unto their king' from the Jordan to Jerusalem (II Sam 20:2, AV).

Many today scorn the idea of a close, dependent relationship between husband and wife. They claim that it stifles the development of character, and restricts the freedom of the partners in a marriage. They advocate a lifestyle which might be dubbed 'married singles,' in which two people who are married continue to follow their own independent lives while sharing the same roof and the same bed. Not surprisingly, such marriages often fail, for selfishness lies at their heart.

The world's plan is to guard oneself against being vulnerable, even in marriage. God's plan is to trust and be open. The world urges, 'Get even! Hold on to hurt and resentment! Keep the score!' God encourages, 'Take the risk!' The world demands, 'Nag, criticise, manipulate, domineer.' God tells us to affirm, to build up and to free each other, in marriage as in all our other relationships.

Marital failure stems from a failure to leave and a failure to cleave. Leaving involves far more than the formal giving away of the bride in the wedding service. Cleaving, similarly, demands the forsaking of all others, the giving of lifelong comfort and support, 'for better, for worse, for richer, for poorer, in sickness and in health, to love and to cherish … according to God's holy law.' We make our vows and we must keep them, or we undermine the fabric on which our society is built.

CHAPTER 10

Marriage and Sex

THE third great act of marriage, after betrothal and the handing over of the bride to the groom, is sexual union. For centuries, objective evidence was required that this had taken place. In Old Testament times, and still among Bedouin tribes today, the bridal pair retired to a nuptial tent or chamber at the end of the wedding festivities to make love together while lying on a clean, white sheet. Blood on the sheet in the morning indicated that the bride had been a virgin, and provided evidence of consummation. These tokens of her virginity were then kept by the bride's parents to protect her against false accusations later in life (see Deut 22:13–19). In Europe, into the seventeenth and eighteenth centuries, wedding celebrations ended with 'bedding the bride.' The bridal pair retired to the nuptial chamber and the guests assembled to see them lying in bed together! Depending on social status, the guests were sometimes very reluctant to leave! Modern high jinks on a couple's departure for their honeymoon are the last surviving relic of this ancient custom.

Without sexual union there can be no marriage. Any who are legally married and then, for any reason, fail to consummate, may have the marriage annulled. This is not the same as divorce. They remain single people, for they have never been fully married in the first place.

Contrary to Christian opinion at various times in the history of the church, Bible writers in Old and New Testament times have always had a positive approach to married sex. The Song of Songs openly delights in erotic love. When writing to the Corinthians, Paul urges husbands and wives to fulfil their marital duties together. Their bodies do not belong to themselves alone but to each other. Therefore they should not deprive each other, except by mutual consent and for a time, to devote themselves to prayer. Then they should come together again lest Satan tempt them through lack of self-control (I Cor 7:1–5). The writer of the Letter to the Hebrews insists, 'Marriage should be honoured by all, and the marriage bed kept pure' (Heb 13:4).

On the other hand, Bible writers are unanimous in condemning all forms of sexual activity outside marriage. In ancient Israel the penalty for adultery was death by stoning (see Deut 22:20–30). Paul warned the Corinthians, 'Do not be deceived: Neither the sexually immoral ... nor adulterers, nor male prostitutes, nor homosexual offenders ... will inherit the kingdom of God' (I Cor 6:9,10). After extolling the virtues of married love, the writer to the Hebrews adds, 'God will judge the adulterer and all the sexually immoral' (Heb 13:4).

Modern attitudes

Katharine was married, half a century ago, to a prominent German 13 years her senior. From the start, she was acutely disappointed. Although her husband aroused her sexually she never experienced orgasm. Inadequately educated in sexual matters, she only sensed that something was wrong; night after night she lay bereft and desolate in bed while her husband slept soundly beside her. Neither his rapid advance in German society, nor the arrival of two beautiful daughters allayed Katharine's growing sense of frustration and exasperation. Because she could no longer honour her husband, she felt cheated out of a life and a career of her own. When he refused to sacrifice his position after the rise of Hitler, she could bear him no more. Just before the war, she brought the children to England and the marriage was dissolved.

As Katharine shared her feelings with other young married women, she discovered she was not alone. Many of them were also sexually unfulfilled. They too felt cheated, and trapped in a lifelong union to which they had rashly committed themselves. One of Katharine's friends discovered she had married a homosexual. When she left him six months after the wedding she was blamed and shunned by friends, neighbours and relatives; out of loyalty and loving kindness to her husband she said nothing.

After the war, Katharine enjoyed a long and satisfying relationship with a new partner. Although they never married, she learned from him the joys of marriage. How much more sensible it would be, she thought, for men, and particularly women, to gain sexual experience before they married. How many pitfalls they could avoid if they could know, before committing themselves finally to each other, that they could be happy and satisfied together in bed.

In time, Katharine's eldest daughter grew up and married. A virgin on her wedding night, she married a man with no sexual experience whatsoever. Although they had three children, the marriage was unsatisfactory and ended in breakdown. Later, she lived with another man for five years before marrying him. Of this second marriage Katharine says, 'I have rarely seen a more happily married couple.'

'To expect the girl to go into marriage as a virgin is just folly,' Katharine insists. 'There is so much that can go wrong with the physical relationship that I have become quite clear in my mind that no girl should allow herself to become engaged till she has lain with her man and found joy, peace and release in it. A marriage will rarely break down if the two are good lovers — on the other hand, if they are not, it is a heart-rending misery sticking together out of a sense of duty. This is shocking, considering what a bond of love, joy and peace marriage is meant to be in the mind of a loving God.' Thirty years ago, Katharine described in her autobiography the breakdown of her marriage, the dark night of her soul which followed, and her discovery of Christ.[1] From it, she received hundreds of sympathetic and supportive replies, many of them from wives of clergy...

Katharine is a Christian. For over forty years she has been aware of God. Now, in old age, she is more conscious of him than ever. She has no time for the excesses of the permissive society. And there is undoubtedly much in what she says. Virginity at marriage and wholehearted commitment to Christ are no automatic guarantees of an easy and blissful time, as Penny and Mike discovered.[2] Conversely, many come to marriage sexually experienced and after living together, and do go on to live happily and satisfyingly with each other.

Although sincerely held, Katharine's views are typical of the humanist ideas which have swept through Western society over the past thirty years, bringing profound changes in human behaviour in their wake. In sexual and marital behaviour, they are undermining the whole basis of Christian standards on which our society has been built. Although some, like Katharine's daughter, may claim success and happiness, countless others have found only misery and distress. By example and teaching, we must proclaim the love and law of Christ to all who will hear. We must offer his forgiveness to all who fail. After writing of God's exclusion of the immoral from his kingdom, Paul adds, 'And that is what some of you were. But you were washed, you were sanctified, you were justified in the name of the Lord Jesus Christ and by the Spirit of our God' (I Cor 6:11).

Sex before marriage

Nowhere is Christian morality currently under stronger attack than in this whole area of premarital sexual behaviour among the young. When I started teaching in secondary schools in 1961 and began to give lessons in personal relationships, I was frequently asked, 'Is it wrong,' or, 'Why is it wrong to have sex before marriage?' Around 1970, the question suddenly changed: 'When should you have sex?' Ever since, my answer, 'When you get married,' has been met with scorn

[1] Katharine Trevelyan, *Fool in Love*.
[2] See ch. 4.

and disbelief. The very idea that sex is for marriage just does not enter the thinking of many of the rising generation of young people. The more we thunder against the evils of promiscuity the less notice anyone takes. If we retreat into totally Christian ghettoes, raising our children in Christian schools, regulating their friends as they grow up, eschewing all secular influences from television and literature, we not only lose contact with the world Christ came to save, but we also expose our maturing young people to all the devastation of culture-shock when external circumstances and natural rebellion force them out into the big, wide world.

Pessimistically, I see in the chaos around us the collapse of society and the disintegration of a secularised church, and then I think of the great revivals of the past. I recall how the Spirit of God has touched individuals, towns, whole nations and continents, changing human lives and attitudes and restoring fallen humanity in order to call a holy people to himself. And I pray that he will do it again in our hedonistic, self-destructive society of the late twentieth century. And while revival tarries, we must have done with half-hearted Christianity, dreary worship, out-of-date language, decrepit buildings and insipid fellowship which has lost all contact with the cultural aspirations of the younger generation. Only then, when our faith is demonstrably real and shorn of all hypocrisy, when our love is undimmed and displayed in action, will young people listen to us when we set before them Christ's glorious purpose for their bodies and their lives.

For the big lie about premarital sex is that it affirms our sexuality. It does not; it perverts it and may destroy it. Whatever else it is, premarital sex is not the same as married sex. Therefore, despite Katharine's assertion, it cannot tell us whether we and our partners are suited to marriage or not.

For a start, sex before marriage is sex without commitment. That, for many, is its whole point. If we do not like it, or if we dislike our partner, we can change and find somebody else. So we exploit our partner for our own gratification, or we run the risk of being exploited in turn. Many do feel hurt and used after sexual encounters. They may withdraw from sexual activity altogether for fear of being hurt again, or they may use their bodies even more selfishly, with little or no regard for the feelings of others. Either way, our sexuality is distorted, for once we have become used to a variety of sexual partners, we shall find it all the harder to settle with one when we marry.

Couples with a serious relationship and those who are intending to marry would probably deny that they are using each other if they sleep together. But even engaged couples are not fully and finally committed to each other. If they were, they would be married. Engagement is the final period of preparation, the trial period of suitability for marriage. But it is not marriage. Until the last moment, the final step of total commitment can be avoided. Therefore, if they have intercourse together, they may still feel they have compromised their relationship, and spoiled what was waiting for them.

Because sex before marriage lacks commitment, it also lacks security. When we come together in marriage, we know we shall keep on doing so, even if our first efforts are awkward, clumsy and disappointing. They often are, of course, and here is another of the permissive society's big lies; sex is always great, exciting and thrilling. Many find to their cost that the opposite is the case. The art of sexual expression and arousal has to be learned, and the best place to learn it is within the security of marriage. Because we are committed to each other, we keep on trying, and most of us, in time, overcome our initial difficulties. We succeed, because we are secure in our trust in each other.

For some, lack of security may make their sexual experiences exciting, but this again only highlights the difference between married and unmarried sex. In the long term, it is doubtful if we can ever find sex truly satisfying without security. Sexual satisfaction involves far more than the ability to achieve mutual orgasm. We need to know that we love ech other and always will. Without that, we are likely to be left feeling lonely and desolate, rejected by the very experience which should have affirmed us in the depths of our being.

Sex before marriage is also sex without children. It has to be, so again, our experience is not that of married people. Either we risk it, and hope that children will not follow, or else we use a contraceptive. Efficient contraception is supposed to have made sex before marriage all right. Unfortunately, we do not seem to be very efficient at using it. Large numbers of illegitimate children continue to be born. Many couples still have to get married, while a soaring number of abortions, with all their damaging physical and emotional consequences, apparently takes care of the remaining mistakes. Barrier contraceptives are notoriously inefficient in the hands of the unmarried and inexperienced and most unmarried women who go on the pill only do so after sexual activity without precautions, or with unreliable ones.

Contraception, however, is not really the point. The intention to avoid children makes sex before marriage different from married sex. Within marriage, physical union both makes us one and enables us to bear children. Within the totality of our married experience we may regulate the bearing of children, but, as we have argued, we may not deliberately exclude it altogether. And herein lies the essential difference between married and unmarried sex. Children must not be born from unmarried sex. If married people find they are expecting an unplanned child, there is no shame, nor embarrassment, and usually, no overwhelming problem.

We cannot separate sex from childbearing, however hard we may try, and however efficient our contraceptives may be. Something deep within us longs to make us one with another, and longs to make another from our union. This is why sex before marriage distorts our sexuality. We fear a child from our sexual activity. But women, particularly, probably long to have one too. This tension, between wanting and not wanting a child, affects our sexual experience. Perhaps it explains why so many unmarried women risk sex without contraception and why, when the child is born, so many keep it, even though they may not marry the father.

If we separate sex from marriage, when, to return to my pupils' question, do we start? Do we wait until we are engaged, or maybe until we intend to become engaged? Why not have sex to see if we should become engaged? Why not have it to see if we are sexually compatible with each other? Why not have sex with our current boyfriend or girlfriend? Why not have it, as we take our first cigarette or our first drink, to prove we have grown up?

There is, in fact, no answer to the question. Allow sex before marriage and we are cast adrift on an uncharted sea with no warning of rocks and quicksands which may lure us to destruction. One rock is guilt. Despite the assertion of the permissive lobby, sex outside marriage makes us feel guilty. If we persist, our guilt may subside, often only to rise again in middle life bringing frigidity and impotence in its wake.[1]

Often, it does not wait so long. Between the ages of 18 and 25, Rosemary had three steady boyfriends with each of whom she slept. 'I came to feel so guilty,' she admits. 'The relief when I became a Christian and knew I was forgiven was unbelievable!' Gordon similarly became disgusted with himself at the number of girls he took to bed. He, too, found peace only through conversion to Christ.

Brian and Shirley were students far away from home. They fell deeply in love and, although they were Christians, began to make love together. When they found they were expecting a child, they married but, although fully committed to each other, soon found their relationship clouded with guilt. Fortunately, they went to see their minister and made a clean breast of their behaviour. He pointed them to the cross, and then drew a line with chalk across his vestry floor. Together, the three of them stood on one side of the line, signifying the past with all its failure and guilt. Then they stepped across the line into the freedom and forgiveness which only Christ can give, leaving the past behind, crucified with Christ on the cross. Only in this way was their marriage saved, allowing them to face the future together.

There is forgiveness with Christ. His blood does wash us clean of all sin, and that includes sexual sin. Through faith in him we are counted as righteous in the eyes of a holy God. He is our peace, our joy and our

---

[1] See Tim and Beverly LaHaye, *The Act of Marriage,* pp 124f, 162f.

wisdom. I believe he not only forgives our failure, but also restores our virginity when we come and confess to him. Christians are not kill-joys, repressing their natural urges and forcing that repression in others. They are those who have submitted to the Lordship of Christ, creator and ruler of the universe. They have become obedient to his law of love, and they avoid sex before marriage in order that their marriages may be built on solid foundations, and reflect his love to the world.

Living together

'Why don't you get married?' I asked a young woman who was openly living with her boyfriend. 'Because my parents don't want us to,' she replied, 'until we can afford to buy and furnish a house of our own. Anyway, we don't need to get married in order to express our relationship with each other.' 'But are you planning to marry next year,' I pressed. 'Why, if your relationship is perfectly satisfactory as it is?' 'My parents want me to have a white wedding,' came the rather subdued answer. So the hypocrisy of an older generation turns a blind eye on the behaviour of the young, perfectly satisfied if everything seemingly turns out right in the end. More disturbingly, the couple, their parents, the minister and the congregation apparently saw nothing untoward in their living-together situation, nor in the fact that they were active church members at the time.

Living together has undoubtedly grown in popularity, along with widespread changes in attitudes and in society. After all, if it is all right to sleep together, why not live together? If we need to sleep together to see if we are compatible before we marry, why not go the whole hog and find out if we can live happily together as well? So, more and more couples have taken this route to marriage, and for many, like Katharine's daughter, it has apparently worked. 'All of my friends who lived together,' someone else told me, 'subsequently married, and their marriages are working out.'

What then has happened, for living together to become as popular as it has? Not so long ago couples who 'lived tally' had their windows broken by neighbours. Names were called when they walked down the street. Employment was denied. No respectable man or woman would speak to them. And if children came along, they also suffered taunts and isolation.

Social mobility has been a big factor. We no longer live, grow and die in the same locality, generation after generation, as we once did. If strangers from another town move in next door, who knows whether they are married or not? And if they are not, what does it matter? We do not know their families, they do not mean anything to us, and, as for sending them to Coventry, they probably want little, if anything, to do

70

with us either.

Large numbers of young people, particularly those in the higher social and educational brackets, now leave home towards the end of their teens to complete their education in distant cities. There they live in mixed residential accommodation with total freedom to work out their relationships. Once they are qualified, they move again to take up employment, living in flats and bedsitters, sharing houses, free from parental and social restraint. Why should a young man and woman keep two flats going, when they can live just as cheaply in one and save all the harder for their wedding? Why not buy a house together, before the price rises in two years' time? If things fail to work out, well, they can withdraw before the final knot is tied.

Marriage breakdown itself has also encouraged couples to live together. Melanie's father was a philanderer. Every time he bought a new sports car his wife knew he had found a new girl-friend. Bravely, she tried to make the marriage work. Melanie and two other children came along. Mother struggled with limited means to bring up the family, while father lived it up with the latest passion in his life. In the end, a traumatic divorce occurred leaving mother financially impoverished, while father continued his life of idle luxury. Melanie will not risk that for herself. What is the point of marriage, she argues, when people do not keep their promises anyway? So she keeps her job, and with it her financial independence, along with what she claims is a deeply satisfying relationship with her live-in lover. Should the relationship turn sour, either is free to leave at any time. Emotional hurt may follow, but the expense and trauma of divorce will at least be avoided.

'Marriage is the best thing I never did!' Colin said to me one day. 'All my married friends are miserable!' So he lives in his own house, rents part of it out to lodgers, and enjoys a succession of girl-friends who live with him for varying periods of time. He thinks he is enjoying himself. The media think so too, with their constant glamorisation of the love lives of the rich and famous, who seem to take and discard each other at will. And however hard we try, as Christians, to live in God's way and obey his commands, the attitude of the world rubs off. We envy the subjects of the gossip columns with their wealth and their fun. The arguments seem so persuasive. Why should I not sleep with my girl-friend or boy-friend and live with them for a while to see if we are suited to each other? Everybody else does. Why should we be the odd ones out?

Unfortunately, living together suffers from all the drawbacks of sleeping together, and more. For a start, it is not married life. All those I have ever met who are living together insist on this; 'we are not married.' How then can it be a reliable guide to suitability for marriage? Not surprisingly, a significant proportion of those who live together separate after they have married. Although they lived happily together they were not suited to marriage, because marriage is a different way of living.

Living together is usually life without children. Of course, most married couples delay starting a family, but live-in couples must prevent it. Therefore, their relationship is directed inwards. It is self-satisfying rather than creative. Therefore, it is not marriage. Indeed, the growing desire for children often moves live-in couples to marry. Yet they rarely realise that the arrival of a family will change them and their relationship radically. Like the couple who have to get married, they will have to adjust to marriage and parenthood at the same time.

More seriously, living together lacks commitment, or each of the partners brings a different level of commitment to the relationship. The couple have not promised to be husband and wife together 'till death us do part.' Each knows that either can leave at any time. Many do. In 1977, in America a 75 per cent breakdown rate in living-together relationships was reported. In such situations, the emotional stress is equal to divorce. Indeed, it may be worse, because the abandoned partner does not enjoy the same legal protection as he or she would if they were married.

Many live-in couples deny that their relationship suffers from a lack of commitment. 'We are committed to each other, and do not need a piece of paper to prove it,' they say. But is they are so committed, why do they shrink from one further piece of tangible evidence, the wedding certficate. Their refusal to marry demonstrates their lack of total commitment.

Because of their lack of commitment, couples who live together often suffer from insecurity. Sue is a midwife in a large maternity unit. She and one of the surgeons are living together and buying a house. Sue wants to get married, but her partner does not, so she is always trying to think of ways of pleasing him so that he will marry her. She is committed, he is not, so their relationship is fraught with uncertainty.

Married love is sacrificial. It gives everything, even life itself, for the benefit and well-being of the spouse. But live-in love is selfish. It satisfies me now, and when it fails, I can find someone else. Of course, many marriages are selfish too and break down. But despite the rising divorce rate, many, many marriages are deeply enriching and satisfying. They are not breaking down, and are providing their partners with lifelong security in a way that live-in relationships never can.

During the late 1960s, sociologist Nancy Clatworthy became intrigued with the phenomenon of living together. She saw it as 'a bold new step, a sensible thing, an extension of the old process of going steady and being pinned.' Couples reported to her how glad they were to be involved in the arrangement and how wonderful it was. Initially, she believed them.

Later, Clatworthy conducted detailed questionnaires among several hundred young people in and around Ohio State University in Columbus. When she analysed the answers and compared those who were living together or who had lived together before marrying with those who were married and had not lived together first, she rapidly changed her mind.

'Surface answers in favour of living together were not supported by underlying feelings. Among those who had married but had lived together first, the most common problems were in the areas of adjustment, happiness and respect... Couples who live together before marriage disagree more often on finances, friends, and demonstration of affection than couples who marry before cohabiting.'

Even more surprisingly, Clatworthy discovered that married couples who had lived together were less well adjusted sexually than those who had not. 'Couples who had lived together before marriage disagreed about sex more often. You'd assume that this would be an area that could be satisfactorily resolved in a living-together period. Apparently it isn't.'[1]

Clatworthy's study does not seem to have detected feelings of guilt. But that too is often present when couples move in together. John met Vanessa at work. Through speaking to her of his Christianity he learned she was going through a divorce. Their relationship gradually deepened and now they are living together. Although John claims they are very happy he admits to having "nagging doubts as to whether I am failing God, or whether I would be failing her if we split up." I am concerned that Christians are failing John, for his minister happily allows him to remain active in church life while fully aware of his equivocal relationship.

Marriage alternatives and the law of God

Since the end of the Second World War, more and more couples in Western society have been sleeping together and living together before getting married. If the arguments of the humanists are correct, we should therefore be enjoying a higher degree of marital happiness than ever before. In fact, the opposite is the case. Sexually transmitted diseases are rampant and appearing in new and frighteningly unexpected forms. The incidence of one-parent families is widespread. Abortion has become a growth industry. Between three and five out of ten marriages are ending in divorce. If the strait-laced attitudes of a century ago condemned countless people to a lifetime of sexual and marital misery, we cannot claim to be doing any better today.

[1] For a full account of Clatworthy's study and conclusions see Charles and Bonnie Remsberg, *The case against living together*, *Seventeen* Magazine, USA, November 1977.

73

Sleeping and living together cannot prepare people adequately for marriage because they distort God's purpose for the marriage relationship. Sex before marriage may not be married sex, but because of the one-flesh principle it 'marries' those who become involved. They become one flesh. This is one reason why many couples who sleep together find it so hard to separate afterwards, even though they know they are not really suited to each other. Having been joined they cannot bear the prospect of being parted. So they stay together, hoping everything will work out, often only to be broken and disillusioned when the inevitable breakdown finally comes.

Sexual compatibility is not the yardstick for happy and successful marriage. It is the ability to relate and communicate at the deepest levels of our personalities in every area of our lives that matters. When we marry, physical union cements the relationship, but in a growing relationship of love, intercourse can distort the natural process of sharing together whereby we discover whether we are suited to each other or not.

Preaching in All Souls, Langham Place in the heart of London in June 1979, Canon Michael Baughen, now Bishop of Chester, declared, "Sexual commitment is always intended to be the climax following the marriage commitment and not the forerunner of it. If it is the forerunner, then I want to say to you that I think your loss is for all your marriage, for *all* your marriage. You can't go back on it. In one sense I think you always lose the highest view of sex that God wants you to have. You've settled for second best, because it can never have for you again that special touch of being the final seal on your love commitment which was expressed publicly in marriage."[1]

If we sleep together before we marry we come as 'married' people to our wedding. If we sleep with someone and then marry someone else we are effectively committing adultery, because through our former union we were 'married' to them. Of course we can be forgiven, of course we can be cleansed, but we shall carry the effects of our behaviour with us to the end of our days, because any sexual union always affects us permanently.

If sex before marriage distorts God's purpose for two people who are growing in love, living together does so even more. Trial marriage is a contradiction in terms, because marriage is for life and we cannot have a trial life. We do not have trial babies to see how we score at being parents. Babies are human lives, and once they are born we are committed to bringing them up.

Once we live together we are married, whether we like it or not. John and Vanessa are married despite their assertion to the contrary.

[1] Michael A. Baughen, *Let marriage be held in honour*, All Souls' Papers, catalogue number C22/2b/ASP.

John *is* failing God, for he is guilty of fornication, however sincere and well-meaning he may be. He is also failing Vanessa, for he is not loving her with whole-hearted commitment, as Christ loves his church. But they are married, and if they separate they will suffer all the emotional consequences of a broken marriage.

Hazel is similarly married. She works for a large, international company. Four years ago she began an affair with a married man who has two children. She knows the deceit involved in the relationship is wrong, but denies that 'our relationship and the love-making which fulfils it could be wrong. We are committed to each other, just as much as he is committed to his wife and children. We take the greatest care that his family should never find out, and ensure that no more time and money is spent on me than on his family. I am single and hope to remain so — it suits my temperament so that I can give the rest of my time to my work and to the Church — I know I could not find the energy I need without the support and love of this man. I have no intention of taking him from his wife.'

In fact, to all intents and purposes, Hazel has become a second wife, and a very unsatisfactory one at that. If she is totally committed to her man, he is sharing her with another, and deceiving his first wife into the bargain. Hazel's love is self-indulgent, enjoyed purely for her own support and benefit; it can never be creative as it should. She is also a hypocrite, for in the same breath that she justifies her own adulterous relationship she can be heard to decry the low moral standards of the girls with whom she works, and those of their parents. What's sauce for the goose is sauce for the gander!

In 1976, Tim and Beverly LaHaye published the results of a sexual survey they had conducted among 3,500 men and women who had attended their Family Life Seminars across the United States. When they compared their findings with a similar survey, taken about the same time, of 100,000 women by *Redbook* magazine they drew some remarkable conclusions. 'Over the long years of matrimony, Christians ... experience a mutually enjoyable love relationship ... engage in the act of marriage more frequently and with greater satisfaction than do non-Christians in our society.' When they asked, 'If you had to live your life over again, what one thing would you do differently?', the most popular answer they received was, 'I would not have engaged in premarital sex.' They commented, 'It is a sad paradox that so many of those who have rejected or neglected God in their pursuit of sexual freedom and happiness often live miserable lives, whereas the Christian, who is often despised or ridiculed as being too "straight," enjoys the very things the non-Christian is seeking.'[1]

[1] See Tim and Beverly LaHaye, *The Act of Marriage,* chapter 9, *Sex Survey Report.*

We do not need to sleep together, or to live together, in order to learn if we are suited to marriage. If we try, we may fail, for apart from the natural drawbacks discovered by Nancy Clatworthy and others, we shall also be breaking God's law and distorting his purpose for our lives.

Soon after Katharine Trevelyan married so unhappily, Grace began '42 years of supremely happy marriage... Married just before my twenty-third birthday to a man nine months younger than myself, I was totally ignorant of all sexual matters. My future husband and I experienced that wonderful love at first sight so glamorised by the romantic novelists. From our first meeting I knew that for me there would never be another man, and I learned very soon after that it had been the same for him.

'We were married within nine months, and because he was so gentle, tender and understanding in those early days together, we had a perfect physical marriage. During the months of courting we were often in a situation where intercourse could have taken place, and both of us were emotionally inclined. However, we were restrained by what I can only describe as an ingrained feeling of not wishing to sully what promised, and indeed proved, to be a perfect union to come.

'I know I'm old fashioned and a "square," but I also know that our restraint in those wonderful early days of our courtship was the firm basis on which our marriage stood for 42 years of complete trust and happiness.

'I hope ... that an old woman's experience may make one or two young people think twice. Many blame present-day stress and strains for slackness, but, marrying in 1929, we had stresses and strains too.'[1]

[1]   Letter to the Editor, *Church Times*, 23 March 1984.

CHAPTER 11

The Constitution of Marriage

In the stage musical *West Side Story*, the boy and the girl from rival gangs who fall in love with each other, one night break into a large department store in New York. With youthful zest and exuberance, they rampage through the store, overturning one display unit after another. Finally, they arrive in the bridal department. There the girl selects a head-dress from the stand and places it on her head. Holding hands, the two make their wedding promises together, then they retire to the bedroom department to consummate their love for each other.

Are they, or are they not married? Great confusion exists, in society and among Christians at the present time, concerning the actual constitution of marriage. In many minds, marriage is equated with the wedding and with the legal confirmation of the wedding, the marriage certificate. According to this view, you are not married until you have your marriage lines. All the emphasis is on the document. Understandably, many are reacting against this facile view. Recognising the importance of relationship they are despising marriage as a piece of paper. So, as we have seen, they are simply moving in together, sometimes for the rest of their lives.

Some Christians are placing the focus of marriage on sexual union. They are over-emphasising the one-flesh principle to the point where they are insisting that once a couple have been physically united they are married, and they are demanding that such couples ratify their marriages in civil or church weddings. In some societies, this is the way marriage works. Among Indians of the Chaco in South America, for example, a boy who takes a girl into the forest is married to her; they live as husband and wife thereafter. A married man who takes a woman into the forest is guilty of adultery and is punished accordingly.

Now, undoubtedly, as we have also seen, sexual union is vital to marriage; without it there is no marriage. Yet to demand that sex and marriage are one and the same is to distort one's understanding of both. Sex before marriage does not constitute marriage but fornication. To pressure couples into marrying because they have slept together is to invite disaster later in life when they will almost certainly demand to break free from a relationship they never wanted anyway. Such couples should be encouraged to seek God's forgiveness. Maybe they will subsequently marry, but that must be because they want to, not because they are forced to.

Marriage involves leaving one's parents, cleaving to one's wife or husband and becoming one flesh. The three elements must always occur for marriage to take place. At one level marriage is deeply personal: the couple agree to become husband and wife together. At another level, it is a family affair. Whether they are formally given away or handed over or not, two people leave their families and start a new one. The extent to which they continue to relate to their original families varies according to social status and social conditions at the time, but families are always involved. At yet another level, marriage is public business. Society has to know who is married to whom. Children must know who their parents are, not only for their emotional well-being, but to be protected from incestuous unions when they grow up. The couple in *West Side Story* were not married, for their vows were taken in private with none to hear.

In the small village communities of the Chaco, where everyone knows what everyone else is doing, leading a girl into the forest is sufficient public testimony to the fact that marriage is happening. In antiquity, the bridal procession served the same purpose. Modern photographs are similarly important. In addition, advanced urban societies have always found it necessary to regulate and control the conduct of weddings, and to provide a legal document as evidence that they have taken place.

But the ceremony and the document do not constitute the marriage. The combined acts of consenting together, of leaving one's parents and of becomng one, make a man and a woman husband and wife. And these can occur without a formal ceremony and legal ratification. In England, we recognise the 'common law' marriage. Strictly speaking, the term is a misnomer, for there is no actual recognition of marriage in English Common Law. But we accept that, to all intents and purposes, a man and a woman can become husband and wife and can raise a family without ever having their marriage legally conducted and registered. Marriage is what they do, in leaving their parents and setting up home together, rather than anything a priest or civil registrar may do to them. Conversely, we annul the legal document if we discover, for example, that the couple have not freely consented to marry, or that they are closely related and should never have married in the first place, or that they have married under the age of eighteen without their parents' consent, or that they have never consummated their marriage. Marriage is not what happens in church, but what happens in bed between a man and a woman who have freely decided to leave their parents to become husband and wife.

None of this is to decry the importance of church and civil weddings. For the vast majority of people they are, and will continue to be, a necessary part of the process of getting married. But they are not vital, and it is important that we remember this when we come to discuss the vexed question of divorce and remarriage. If marriage is indissoluble (see Chapter 5) we need to be quite sure what constitutes marriage, or we may find we are marrying some who are married already, and denying marriage to others who qualify.

The threefold pathway to marriage: consent, leaving parents and becoming one, with a ceremony somewhere between the second and third paths, is rarely neat and tidy. Parental arrangements for a suitable partner may blur a couple's consent. Inadequate housing or social customs may force newly-weds to live in a parental home. In the Caribbean, with its long, sad history of slavery, it is almost normal for couples to live together and raise a family for years before having a proper wedding. Men and women are always likely to anticipate their marriage sexually. This is not to justify sex before marriage and living together, but simply to take a realistic view of human behaviour. And the longer a couple develop a sexual relationship with each other, the more closely it approximates to marriage, whether they legally marry or not.

Individual, family and society; three levels at which marriage takes place. Almost every society also recognises a fourth, the Divine. God, or the gods, are nearly always involved as well, because in becoming husband and wife, a man and a woman reflect the Divine image. We must now consider how the Christian church has recognised this level, how it has developed its marriage ceremonies, and how it continues to conduct weddings and regulate marriage at the present time.

CHAPTER 12

Jewish Rites

THE Bible gives no directions for the conduct of weddings. They are not, apparently, the concern of the state or the religious authorities, but of the families and individuals involved. So, in the Old Testament, we find allusions to weddings taking place as they did throughout the rest of the ancient world. Betrothals, bridal processions, feasts and consummation were all necessary elements in Israelite weddings as they were elsewhere.

Nevertheless, their strong sense that marriage was ordained by God from the beginning and that he gave children as the fruit of the womb, meant that God's blessing was invoked on married couples from the earliest times. When Rebekah agreed to accompany Eliezer and marry Isaac her family blessed her and said,

> Our sister, may you increase
>   to thousands upon thousands;
> may your offspring possess
>   the gates of their enemies (Gen 24:60).

The Song of Songs, possibly composed to be sung during the bridal procession of Solomon or some other king, was accepted as divinely inspired and was included in the scriptures. Psalm 45 is another royal wedding song, prophetically anticipating the Messianic Bridegroom (see Ps 45:6,7; cf. Heb 1:8,9). Psalm 127 returns to the theme of blessing:

> Sons are a heritage from the LORD,
>   children a reward from him.
> Like arrows in the hands of a warrior
>   are sons born in one's youth.
> Blessed is the man
>   whose quiver is full of them (Ps 127:3–5).

Tobias and the angel

After the Jews had been carried into captivity by the Babylonians, they told the story of Tobias and the angel. Sent by his father Tobit to collect some money deposited in a distant city, Tobias hired a man to accompany him who was Raphael, the angel, in disguise. On the way, they stayed with Tobias' relatives, Raguel and Edna. They had a daughter, Sarah, who had been married seven times before, but each time, on her wedding night, an evil spirit had attacked the bridegroom and killed him before the marriage could be consummated.

Under the Levirate law, as a male relative, Tobias was obliged to marry Sarah. Raphael asked Raguel for her hand in marriage on his behalf and told him how to exorcise the evil spirit when they retired into the bridal chamber. All went according to plan. Tobias survived his wedding night, retrieved his father's money, and returned home with his new-found wife, amidst great rejoicing.

Tobias' story is found in the Apocrypha, a collection of writings added to the Old Testament and accepted as scriptural by some Christians. Its importance lies not in its truth or authority or otherwise, but on the light it sheds on the development of Jewish wedding rituals in the period preceding the birth of Christ. When Tobias and Sarah were alone in the bridal chamber together he suggested they pray and beseech the Lord to show them mercy and keep them safe. Tobias said:

> We praise thee, O God of our fathers, we praise thy name
> for ever and ever.... Thou madest Adam, and Eve his wife
> to be his helper and support; and those two were the
> parents of the human race. This was thy word: "It is not
> good for the man to be alone; let us make him a helper like
> him." I now take this my beloved wife, not out of lust but in
> true marriage. Grant that she and I may find mercy and
> grow old together (Tobit 8:5–8 NEB).

In the morning, when Tobias and Sarah were found alive and well, Raguel praised God: "'Praise to thee for the mercy thou hast shown to these two, these only children. Lord, show them mercy, keep them safe, and grant them a long life of happiness and affection'" (Tobit 6:17 NEB).

The Talmud

During and after the Babylonian Exile, from which the story of Tobias comes, Jewish leaders began to expand and apply the law of Moses as recorded in the Old Testament, to cover every eventuality and area of life. Between the second and fifth centuries of the Christian era, the collected work of the rabbis was gathered together and written down in the Talmud. Many of its contents were already hallowed by time, and reflect Jewish beliefs and practice long before the period of their composition.

In the Talmud, marriage is highly organised and more closely regulated than previously. Betrothal lasts for twelve months before its ratification in marriage itself. Single girls marry on Wednesdays, widows on Fridays, thus avoiding fast-days. The couple fast all day and confess their sins. Both wear myrtle crowns, and if the bride is a virgin, she wears a long veil as well. The bridegroom takes the bride in procession to his home for an evening feast with music and dancing. On the threshold of his home, the marriage contract is written down. At the end of the festivities, before the guests disperse and the couple retire together, the bridegroom recites a prayer of seven blessings:

> Blessed art thou, O Lord our God, King of the universe, who creates the fruit of the vine.
> Blessed art thou, O Lord our God, King of the universe, who has created all things to thy glory.
> Blessed art thou, O Lord our God, King of the universe, Creator of man.
> Blessed art thou, O Lord our God, King of the universe, who hast made man in thine image, after thy likeness, and hast prepared unto him, one of his very self, a perpetual fabric. Blessed art thou, O Lord, Creator of man.
> May she who was barren (Zion) be exceeding glad and exult, when her children are gathered within her in joy. Blessed art thou, O Lord, who makes Zion joyful through her children.
> O make these loved companions greatly to rejoice, even as of old thou didst gladden thy creature in the garden of Eden. Blessed art thou, O Lord, who makest bridegroom and bride to rejoice.
> Blessed art thou, O Lord our God, King of the universe, who has created joy and gladness, bridegroom and bride, mirth and exultation, pleasure and delight, love, brotherhood, peace and fellowship. Soon may there be heard in the cities of Judah, and in the streets of Jerusalem, the voice of joy and gladness, the voice of the bridegroom and the voice of the bride, the jubilant voice of bridegrooms from their canopies, and of youths from their feasts of song.
> Blessed art thou, O Lord, who makest the bridegroom to rejoice with the bride.[1]

[1] Quoted in Kenneth Stevenson, *Nuptial Blessing,* p. 245.

Tobias' prayer in the bedroom has become a public prayer, offered by the bridegroom, marking the end of the wedding. Soon it would be taken over by the rabbis, along with the conduct of the marriage ceremony itself. No longer directed by the families, marriage moved into the synagogue where a special canopy was erected to symbolise the bridegroom's house.

By the Middle Ages, following Christian practice, Jewish betrothal and marriage was combined into a single ceremony. A ring or coin was exchanged during the recital of prescribed words. In accordance with the law of the state, the marriage was formally ratified in a legal document.

What then would constitute marriage? Would it be the consent of the couple, the giving of the bride to the groom, or physical consummation? Or again, was the essence of marriage a prescribed ceremony in a prescribed place, presided over by a prescribed person? Christians, also, were to face this question, as we shall see.

CHAPTER 13

From Caesar to Rome

The earliest Christians

The New Testament, like the Old, contains no directions for the conduct of weddings. Marriage, as we have seen, is a recurring topic and Christian standards are established. But the idea of Christian marriage, as opposed to non-Christian marriage, is totally absent.

This, then, leaves us with the fascinating question, how did the earliest Christians marry? And the answer must be, they married like everybody else. Or did they? We surely cannot imagine that those who were washed and sanctified and justified in the name of the Lord Jesus Christ and by the Spirit of our God reverted to pagan fertility rites when it came to getting married.

For Jewish Christians, of course, there was no problem. Their wedding celebrations, as we have seen, were noticeably free from idolatry. Since marriage was a creation ordinance and not a Christian invention, they simply continued to marry in the Jewish way with the bridegroom reciting the Seven Blessings as described in the previous chapter. Soon, the Blessings were adapted to include specifically Christian material. The Gregorian Sacramentary of the sixth century, for example, which, like the Talmud, reflects earlier practice, includes the line, 'O God, you have hallowed marriage by a mystery so excellent that in the marriage bond you prefigured the union of Christ with the Church.'[1]

Gentile Christians similarly must have used the Jewish rite. Most of the very earliest Gentile converts were, of course, God-fearers and proselytes, fully accustomed to Jewish synagogue-worship week by week. They would have little difficulty in accepting Jewish wedding customs when they were married. By the time later generations of Gentiles were coming into the church directly from the society around

[1] Quoted in Kenneth Stevenson, *Nuptial Blessing,* p. 245.

them, the practice of Jewish, now Christian, marriage was firmly established. In marriage celebrations, as in every other area of the Church's worshipping life, all the evidence suggests that the early Christians adapted Jewish rituals, gave them Christian content, and, under the influence of the Spirit of God, set them free from formality and tradition.

For three hundred years the earliest Christians were a threatened minority within the Roman Empire. Practising an illegal religion they were subject to successive waves of increasingly fierce and determined persecution. During these times they met and worshipped in secret. Often, Christian couples must have faced traumatic conflicts of loyalties when they insisted on marrying in the Christian way. Then the support of the family of the church must have meant as much, or more, than the presence of their own families. If a girl's pagan father refused to hand her over to her Christian husband it seemed natural for the elder to do it for him. At the end of the feast, the bridegrooms began to ask one of the elders to recite the Seven Blessings before the guests departed and the couple retired together. Slowly, imperceptibly, weddings were not only Christianised but clericised as well.

In hoc vince!

Early in the year 312 the citizens of Rome waited anxiously as rival armies prepared for battle outside the city. Constantine's long march from York, in Britain, was finished. Maxentius, who had seized the Imperial throne on the retirement of Diocletian, prepared to defend his hard-won crown.

The previous decade had seen unparalleled religious and political turmoil throughout the Empire. Diocletian had unleashed the last, determined attempt to destroy the expanding Christian church. Buildings had been destroyed, books confiscated, Christians dismissed from the army and civil service, while everyone had been required to sacrifice to the Emperor. Entire towns had been massacred in the persecution which followed. Politically, Diocletian's decision to retire had left the Empire ripe for the taking; rival generals had not refused the challenge.

Constantine defeated Maxentius, crossed the Milvian Bridge and entered the Eternal City in triumph. There he declared how, on the night before the battle, he had seen a flaming cross in the sky, encircled by the words, 'In hoc vince!', 'In this [sign], conquer!' Whether he had or not, the long night of persecution and suffering was over. Within a year, Christianity was a legal religion. Within a century, it became the official religion of the Roman Empire.

The fourth century saw Christian growth on a scale undreamed-of in the earlier years of danger and threat. Aided by generous government grants, large and impressive church buildings were erected in every city and town. Christian leaders leaped at the chance to transform society for Christ. Blood sports in the arena were ended and slaves set free. Thousands flocked to the church and were baptized, yet what emerged, in many hearts, was a strange mixture of pagan beliefs and half-taught Christian truths.

Nowhere was the problem of 'Christianising' human behaviour more acute than in the area of marriage. Increasingly, Christian weddings were held in church buildings, instead of in the homes of the couples involved. There, the role of the clergy inevitably grew. Naturally, they seized the opportunity to explain Christian marriage standards to their assembled congregations. The Sevenfold Blessing, originally recited by the bridegroom at the end of the feast, gradually offered instead by an elder, was now re-written with a Christian content and incorporated into the church service itself.

By the end of the century, as we have seen, Christian leaders were describing marriage as a *sacramentum*.[1] By the fifth century, we have the first mention of a 'nuptial mass,' that is, a wedding conducted within the context of a communion service. It is testimony, not only to the sacramental understanding of marriage, but also to the growing importance of the eucharist as the central rite of Christian worship.

Where now lay the heart of marriage? Ancient tradition and Roman law said it lay in the consent of the couple to live as husband and wife. Custom and practice continued to set considerable store in the giving of the bride by her father to the groom. Nature said it lay in the act of intercourse. More and more, Christians were saying it found its focus in the blessing given by the priest to the couple. Without this, marriage could never fully become a reflection of Christ's love for his church. Unless their marriage was sealed with the priestly blessing, Christians could not properly take their place in the body of Christ, enjoying his love and displaying it to others.

Decline and fall

By the seventh century, the Roman Empire was struggling to survive. Tribes from northern Europe were pressing on its borders with increasing ferocity and determination. One area after another declared independence. New empires and dynasties emerged from which are descended the nation states of modern Europe. In the end Rome itself was sacked and destroyed. In the East, the Empire survived, but in the West it disintegrated into chaos and strife.

The situation was similar to that which obtains over large areas of Africa today, where one tribe after another struggles to restore the

[1] See above, p. 29.

broken peace of former colonial rule. Then, as now, the one remaining stable force in society was the Christian church. There alone were peace, honesty and justice. Because its leaders were men of integrity they were frequently entrusted with political as well as religious responsibility. The bishop of Rome in particular, as the one remaining visible expression of the Empire, found that more and more disputes were referred to his jurisdiction. Supposed successors of St Peter responded readily to the new situation; eventually they exercised political as well as religious control over the whole of Europe.

In the middle of the ninth century some false documents[1] were produced which were attributed to Evaristus, the supposed immediate successor of St Peter. They asserted the indissolubility of marriage and required its 'solemnisation' by a priest for it to be truly Christian. Because of their apparent antiquity they were held to have the force of Imperial law; they regulated the church's marriage practice for the next six hundred years.

Marriage was a sacrament, an effective sign of God's grace. Only through the eucharist, received in the nuptial mass, and the priestly blessing, could God's grace be received. Divorce was impossible, and therefore forbidden. If a couple were found to have married within the forbidden degrees of kinship, or if they could prove their marriage had never been consummated, it could be annulled. Gradually, grounds for annulment were extended, but the process was slow and costly, and therefore largely confined to those with influence in the upper reaches of the Church.

Not that universal control over marriage was easily achieved. During the tenth century, the church was granted complete jurisdiction in marital law throughout the Frankish Empire. After the Norman Conquest it received similar rights in England. By the end of the twelfth century its control had extended to the rest of Western Europe. A similar process took place in the East.

Even then, people grudgingly accepted ecclesiastical rule. Child betrothal and clandestine marriage were rife. As late as 1076, Lanfranc in England had to remind laymen to obtain the blessing of the church on their marriages. In 1102 Anselm was objecting to private weddings.[2]

From this period come many of the features of weddings which are still familiar today. Betrothal was incorporated into the marriage ceremony itself; the couple had to give their consent publicly, and be heard to do so. Weddings were held in the church porch (or, for the rich, in the church itself) after due notice, to guard against marriage within the forbidden degrees. A ring had to be exchanged as continuing evidence

[1] The Pseudo-Isidorian Decretals.
[2] See D.J.A. Matthew, *The Norman Conquest,* p. 192.

that the marriage had taken place, and to protect the young bride against abduction. All who disobeyed the church's rule were excommunicated.

Since the Reformation of the sixteenth century, Protestant Christians have found it easy to criticise the mediaeval church for its assumption of political power, for the tyranny it exercised over millions of people whom it left in dark ignorance of the truths of the Gospel. Yet it is not fair to characterise the Christians of this period as power-mad, greedy hypocrites who used the church for their own selfish ends. Some, of course, indeed fell into this trap. Many more were men and women of great godliness. Their grasp of Christian truth was profound. Often, like Francis of Assisi, they saw religious revival among the poorest of the people. Frequently, they were deeply concerned at the abuses which were tolerated in church and society, and actively worked to correct them.

Mediaeval Christians, like all Christians, were children of their age, acting with a mixture of human weakness and failure, and the conscious leading of the Spirit of God. When they defined marriage as a sacrament, an effective sign of the bond between Christ and the church, they did so out of deep desire to see Christ's love displayed in the lives of those who were married. When they insisted on the indissolubility of marriage and used their state-backed power to forbid remarriage, their concern at persistent low standards despite centuries of 'Christianisation' was genuine. When they asserted that the heart of marriage lay in the priestly blessing, their thinking was confined to a closed 'Christian' world, largely unaware of vast numbers of non-Christians who lived beyond its borders. Given the same situation, opportunities and power, many modern Christians would probably respond in the same way.

When Constantine ascended the Imperial throne in 312 it was inconceivable that the *Pax Romana* could ever be broken. When Leo X became bishop of Rome in 1513, the future of the Papal empire seemed similarly assured. But a new storm was about to break, a new cataclysm to shake the heart of Europe. We, in the modern world, are its children and descendants.

CHAPTER 14

Reformation and Renewal

Reformation turmoil

In 1517, when Martin Luther nailed the Ninety-Five Theses to the door of the church in Wittenberg, Europe was ready for reformation. The Christian church had grown fat and lazy, providing an easy route, for those so inclined, to material gain and power. Among the people at large Christian truth had become overlain with mediaeval superstition. To all intents and purposes the way of salvation consisted of regular attendance at Mass, not to receive communion (except three times a year), but to watch the priest, through the screen with his back turned to the congregation, lift the exalted host high above his head. All the services were chanted in Latin, and were therefore totally meaningless to all but a tiny, educated minority. Abuse was rampant. Although priests and members of religious orders had taken vows of celibacy, these were frequently broken and irregular behaviour tolerated. The very word nepotism comes from the practice of mediaeval popes appointing their illegitimate sons, or nephews as they were called, to high office.

Beneath the apparently well-ordered surface of European society, currents of change were beginning to flow. Through the Renaissance, new areas of knowledge were being explored which often conflicted with ecclesiastical dogma. Voyages of discovery were leading to the New World, and opening up new trade routes to the East. The development of printing enabled ideas to spread with greater rapidity than ever before, not only geographically but socially, as the ability to read and the means to do so reached further down the social scale. Politically, the princes of Europe were growing restless under the domination of the Bishop of Rome, and were ready to grasp at any opportunity to assert their independence.

Nevertheless, the Reformation was sparked by the spiritual pilgrimage of one man. Martin Luther, an obscure German monk with a conscience tortured by the supposed enormity of his sins, was appointed Lecturer in the University of Wittenberg. There he gained access to the Bible and was charged with teaching it to his students. There he learned that 'the righteous will live by faith' (Rom 1:17) and not by religious observance. The revelation transformed him from a gloomy, manic depressive, seeking peace of mind through self-flagellation and endless penance, into the liberty of one who knows he is a child of God. When the Papal emissary, John Tetzel, arrived in Wittenberg offering salvation through the purchase of indulgences to pay for the building of St Peter's, Rome, Luther made his historic protest.

Luther had no intention of convulsing Europe; he simply wished to open up academic debate on the abuses associated with the sale of indulgences. But the rejection of his ideas and his subsequent excommunication from the church quickly convinced him that the Bishop of Rome was not the Vicar of Christ on earth, but the Antichrist, intent on turning the people away from the way of salvation. Within a decade he re-established Christian doctrine on the basis of what he found in Holy Scripture rather than in the tradition of the church.

Initially, he retained the mediaeval view that marriage was a remedy for sin, and was scandalized when monks and nuns began to leave the cloisters to marry. However, his own marriage in 1525 to a former nun, Katharine von Bora, and the subsequent birth of their six children, convinced him of the value of the home, rather than the monastery, as a school for character. Thereby, he exalted marriage from the low esteem into which it had fallen, and effectively established the Protestant parsonage.

Doctrinally, Luther rejected the idea that marriage was a sacrament of the church. The state should control matrimonial law, though the church would quite properly continue to conduct weddings on the state's behalf. Like the rest of the liturgy, marriage should be celebrated in the language of the people. Shorn of its eucharistic setting, the Word should be preached instead, providing the couple and the congregation with instruction in godly living.

What Luther did in Germany, John Calvin the lawyer did in France. His monumental *Institutes of the Christian Religion*, constantly revised and expanded throughout his lifetime, became the foundation of Reformed Christianity. Defining a sacrament as 'an external ceremony appointed by God to confirm a promise,' he denied that marriage was anything of the kind.[1] Like Luther, he therefore denied the church's 'cognisance of conjugal causes,' and thus reasserted the state's jurisdiction in marital law. The church should still conduct weddings, but the state should decree who could, and who could not marry.[2] He condemned the church's prohibition of marriage to clergy as, 'contrary to the word of God,' 'contrary to all justice,' and as hav-

[1] John Calvin, *Institutes of the Christian Religion*, Book 4, Ch. 19, para. 34.
[2] *ibid.*, Book 4, Ch. 19, para. 37.

ing 'deprived the Church of fit and honest pastors.'[1]

When Calvin reformed the liturgy he was more thorough than Luther. He not only removed marriage from its eucharistic setting but abolished the ring and the joining of hands. Before the vows were taken the Word was to be preached. As with Luther, the priestly blessing became a prayer that God would bless the newly-married couple. Conscious of the fellowship of the church, Calvin wanted marriage to become a congregational celebration, though in practice it rapidly reverted to an occasional office only attended by the families and friends of those involved. Calvin's Reformation spread to Switzerland, the Low Countries and Scotland, and became the faith of the English Puritans, the founders of Dissent.

In England, the Reformation was a compromise. Its impetus was unashamedly political and was carried through simply to allow King Henry VIII to divorce Queen Catherine and marry Anne Boleyn. During Henry's lifetime episcopal organisation and Catholic practice were preserved intact; doctrinal and liturgical reformation followed later and was largely the work of Thomas Cranmer, Archbishop of Canterbury.

Matrimony was not to be counted as one of the sacraments of the gospel as it had not 'any visible sign or ceremony ordained of God.'[2] But the Solemnization of Matrimony was little more than a variation and translation of the old Sarum rite, stripped of its eucharistic context. In Cranmer's first Prayer Book of 1549, the priestly blessing became a prayer, 'O Lord, bless them both, and grant them to inherit thy everlasting kingdom, through Jesus Christ our Lord,'[3] and this pattern was followed in the subsequent Books to 1662. 'Bishops, priests and deacons, are not commanded by God's Law, either to vow the estate of single life, or to abstain from marriage: therefore it is lawful for them as for all other Christian men, to marry at their own discretion, as they shall judge the same to serve better to godliness.'[4]

Nevertheless, the marriage service did not satisfy the Puritans with their heavy dependence on Calvin. Early in the seventeenth century they petitioned King James I to remove the ring and the joining of hands from the ceremony. When this was refused, marriage remained a problem for them, as the parish church was the only place they could be legally married. Only the Quakers braved persecution to win the right to celebrate marriage within the fellowship of their Sunday morning meeting. With little formal prior notice, weddings occurred almost spontaneously, the whole congregation adding their signatures to the wedding document as witnesses that the marriage had occurred.

[1] *ibid.*, Book 4, Ch. 12, para. 23.
[2] *Book of Common Prayer*, Article XXV.
[3] Quoted in Kenneth Stevenson, *Nuptial Blessing*, p. 247.
[4] *Book of Common Prayer*, Article XXXII.

Eventually, after the upheavals of the Civil War and the Glorious Revolution of 1689, the state accommodated the Puritans, now known as Dissenters or nonconformists. With the advent of civil marriage they then adapted the Prayer Book service to suit their own purposes and meet the minimum requirements of the law. Thus, Christians of all persuasions retained the right to marry any way they chose. When English Christians settled overseas they took this right with them, so that Christian weddings became the norm throughout the English speaking world and many colonial territories.

Civil marriage and Christian renewal

When the Reformers gave jurisdiction in marital affairs back to the state, they paved the way for the civil wedding proper: a non-religious ceremony backed by a legal document and conducted by a registrar. In England, this was introduced in 1857, along with a law of divorce, something which had previously only been possible by private Act of Parliament. At the same time, the Tractarian Movement was making many in the Church of England aware of its Catholic tradition. The indissolubility of marriage and its sacramental character were again being taught. The priestly blessing was being reintroduced into the marriage service by the minister laying his hands on the bride and groom during the prayer of blessing.

During the twentieth century, these trends have gathered pace. More and more people are opting for civil weddings rather than church ones (though church weddings for couples for whom it is a first marriage are still well in the majority), while the Church has become more conscious of its liturgical tradition. The language of all kinds of services has been modernised while their form has reverted to models from the period of the early Fathers.

Roman Catholics have similarly revised their services. Now in the vernacular, they too look to the Fathers for their inspiration. Where both marital partners are Catholics, nuptial mass is celebrated; a shorter service is used where only one partner is a Catholic. Other Christians, such as Methodists and Baptists, have also modernised their marriage services, and some of these follow a similar pattern to the Catholic and Anglican revisions.

Christians are living in a post-Christian age. No longer can they command the support, or even the token allegiance, of the overwhelming majority of the people around them. Nevertheless, substantial sections of the population still come to church at life's great turning points, birth, marriage and death.

On marriage, Christians are deeply divided on the related issues of sacrament and indissolubility. Overall, the rising tide of divorce, in society and within the Church, threatens the lifelong fidelity of Christian marriage. To this issue, and the practical problems it raises we must now turn.

CHAPTER 15

Jesus and Marriage

According to Luke

Between the parables of the Shrewd Manager, and the Rich Man and Lazarus, are recorded a number of apparently unconnected sayings of Jesus. Among them is the cryptic and seemingly uncompromising judgement, 'Anyone who divorces his wife and marries another woman commits adultery, and the man who marries a divorced woman commits adultery' (Luke 16:18). In the opinion of many modern New Testament scholars this constitutes the earliest form of Jesus' teaching on marriage and divorce.[1]

Implicit in Jesus' words is the idea that marriage is intended to be a lifelong exclusive union between a man and a woman. Once a man has married he may not divorce his wife, for if he does, he commits adultery. Neither may a woman divorce her husband, but Luke does not bother to say that, for divorce was the prerogative of men in first century Jewish society.

By his words, Jesus gives men and women an equality in marriage. A man is no more free to put away his wife for someone else than is a woman to change her husband. Therefore a wife is protected from the whim of a capricious husband who tires of her and decides to change her for another. No wonder Luke, with his interest in women and his concern for their welfare, was careful to include Jesus' teaching in his Gospel, even if he found difficulty in placing it in context.

In his judgment, Jesus also challenges the popular idea that divorce encompasses the right to remarry. Indeed, this was regarded as axiomatic among the Jews of his day. A man divorced his wife by declaring to her, 'Behold, thou art permitted to any man.'[2] Jesus says this does not follow. A man who marries a divorced woman also commits

---

[1] See G.J. Wenham, *Gospel Definitions of Adultery and Women's Rights, The Expository Times* 95 (1984), p. 330.
[2] See William A. Heth and Gordon J. Wenham, *Jesus and Divorce*, p. 47.

adultery. Divorce does not destroy the indelible bond forged between a man and a woman when they enter into marriage together.

Therefore, in this one unequivocal sentence Jesus undermines the comfortable assumptions of his day, that men had rights in marriage and women did not, that men could divorce their wives and remarry without breaking God's law, and that marriage need last only as long as a man wished it should. If it is the earliest form of Jesus' teaching on marriage we should not be surprised that it created a furore, not only among the men whose freedom it threatened, but also among the Pharisees who prided themselves on their correct knowledge and application of God's law.

According to Mark

In Mark, Pharisees approach Jesus with the test question, 'Is it lawful for a man to divorce his wife? (Mark 10:2). Perhaps they have heard his teaching, which is now recorded in Luke, and realise it challenges their interpretation of the Law. So they wish to justify themselves, and at the same time to destroy Jesus' claim to speak from God.

Characteristically, Jesus refers the Pharisees to Moses and asks them what he commanded. They refer to Deuteronomy 24:1 and reply, 'Moses permitted a man to write a certificate of divorce and send her away.' Jesus then overrules their answer by insisting that the Mosaic regulation was a concession to human hardness of heart. God's original intention, from the beginning of creation when he made them male and female, was that a man should leave his father and mother and be united to his wife and the two would become one flesh. 'Therefore what God has joined together, let man not separate.'

Afterwards, 'in the house,' the disciples are so astonished at Jesus' reply to the Pharisees' question that they ask him about it again. In a variant of the Lucan judgement, Jesus says, '"Anyone who divorces his wife and marries another woman commits adultery against her. And if she divorces her husband and marries another man, she commits adultery"' (Mark 10:10–12). If Jesus' words in Luke spring from the Jewish culture in which he grew up, in Mark they are directed to the Graeco-Roman world into which his gospel would spread, where, in matters of divorce, wives enjoyed equal rights with their husbands.

Jesus' teaching in Mark is therefore more explicit than in Luke. Marriage was established by God in the beginning. In marriage a man and a woman become one flesh. Their union is indelible and lifelong. Those who divorce and remarry are guilty of adultery. Mosaic legislation in no way compromises God's standard or intention. It constitutes no more than an accommodation to human nature in a fallen world. Indeed, had the Pharisees read Deuteronomy 24 properly they would have understood that it did no more than regulate divorce ('*If* a man marries a woman ... and he writes a certificate of divorce'); its primary purpose was to prevent the remarriage of divorced people who had been married to someone else (see Deut 24:1–4).

Jesus' position in Mark and in Luke is totally consistent. Marriage is a union between one man and one woman. God is not interested in divorce, but in our remaining married to each other. If we divorce and remarry we commit adultery.

According to Matthew

Matthew, like Mark, records Jesus' dispute with the Pharisees, but casts it in rather a different form. They ask the question, "'Is it lawful for a man to divorce his wife for any and every reason?'" (Matt 19:3) In this, they reflect a dispute between followers of two Jewish rabbis, Shammai and Hillel. On the basis of Deuteronomy 24 — 'if a man marries a woman who becomes displeasing to him because he finds something indecent about her' — Shammai had insisted that divorce was only allowed when a wife was convicted of serious sexual misdemeanour. Hillel, on the other hand, had argued that any misdemeanour, even spilling food or talking too loudly, justified divorce.[1] Thus, in Mark, Jesus is asked about the legality of divorce, whereas in Matthew he is asked about the grounds for divorce.

Jesus simply replies by quoting the now familiar passages from Genesis 1 and 2. God made man male and female, therefore a man leaves his father and mother, is united to his wife and the two become one flesh. Since they are no longer two but one, what God has joined together let no man separate (see Matt 19:4–7). So apparently both Shammai and Hillel were wrong. The nature of the marriage was such that any divorce, in whatever circumstances, was contrary to the intention and will of God.

In response, the Pharisees retort, 'Why then did Moses command that a man give his wife a certificate of divorce and send her away?' Moses did not command divorce but permitted it, Jesus rejoins, 'because your hearts were hard. It was not this way from the beginning. Therefore, I tell you that anyone who divorces his wife, *except for marital unfaithfulness*, and marries another woman commits adultery' (Matt 19:8,9).

So Shammai was right after all, or was he? The disciples are so scandalized by Jesus' uncompromising reply that they object, 'If this is the situation between a husband and wife, it is better not to marry' (Matt 19:10). If we cannot divorce our wives for any reason, and then remarry, we are better not marrying at all. To which Jesus replies, 'Not everyone can accept this teaching, but only those to whom it has

[1] See William A. Heth and Gordon J. Wenham, *Jesus and Divorce*, p. 7.

been given. For some are eunuchs because they were born that way; others were made that way by men; and others have renounced marriage because of the kingdom of heaven. The one who can accept this should accept it' (Matt 19:11,12).

With Matthew's account of Jesus' dispute with the Pharisees must be compared his declaration about divorce in the Sermon on the Mount. This is included in a section contrasting Jewish interpretation of the Mosaic Law ('you have heard that it was said to the people long ago') with the new law of the kingdom set out by Jesus himself ('but I tell you'). On divorce, the passage reads, 'It has been said, "Anyone who divorces his wife must give her a certificate of divorce." But I tell you that anyone who divorces his wife, except for marital unfaithfulness, causes her to commit adultery, and anyone who marries a woman so divorced commits adultery' (Matt 5:31,32).

The Deuteronomic law

In their dispute with Jesus, the Pharisees asserted the legality of divorce on the basis of Deuteronomy 24:1: 'he writes her a certificate of divorce, gives it to her and sends her from his house.' Surprisingly, in view of their normal attention to detail, they failed to notice that the law was conditional: '*If* a man marries a woman ... and he writes her a certificate of divorce ... and sends her from his house....' It did not command divorce, but regulated it. It laid down a procedure when it happened. It assumed it would only happen if a husband found 'something indecent' about his wife. It required him to give her a certificate before sending her away. And its main purpose was to forbid the remarriage of a divorced couple if the wife had remarried and been divorced a second time, or even if she had remarried and become widowed: 'her first husband, who divorced her, is not allowed to marry her again after she has been defiled' (Deut 24:4). Remarkably, to modern eyes, once a second marriage had occurred, the first one could not be resumed, for the second marriage 'defiled' the divorced wife. Remarriage to the first husband 'would be detestable in the eyes of the LORD.' So, warns the law, 'do not bring sin upon the land the LORD your God is giving you as an inheritance' (Deut 24:4).

Various reasons have been offered to explain the Deuteronomic ban; it discouraged hasty divorce, it regarded a second marriage as adulterous, or it reflected a man's natural repulsion at resuming intercourse with his wife after she had been unfaithful. But the most convincing view links the law with that on incest in Leviticus 18. Incest among the Canaanites, prior to the Israelite conquest, had 'defiled' the land. Therefore, 'you must not do any of these detestable things' (Lev 18:25,26). From this connection, Heth and Wenham have argued that the remarriage of a divorced couple after one of them has married someone else, constitutes incest. By their first marriage a blood relationship had been created which had made them, not only husband and wife, but close relatives as well. Therefore, if they divorced and one of them married again, remarriage to the original partner was akin to marriage between a brother and sister.[1]

If this conclusion is correct, then Deuteronomy 24 in no way qualifies the earlier teaching of Genesis 1 and 2, but supports it. In marriage, a bond is forced between husband and wife which legal or customary divorce cannot break. No wonder Jesus sets the Deuteronomic provisions aside in his dispute with the Pharisees!

Except for *porneia*

More contentious than the meaning of Deuteronomy, is the way we should understand the Matthaean exception clause, 'except for marital unfaithfulness.' The Greek word is *porneia*, from which we derive the word pornography. The translators of the King James Version of the Bible used the word fornication to convey its meaning, and this was followed in the English Revised Version of the nineteenth century; 'whosoever shall put away his wife, except for fornication, and shall marry another, committeth adultery.' The text was generally understood to allow divorce where one party had been guilty of sexual misconduct. In the twentieth century, the Revised Standard Version and the New English Bible have settled for the more neutral word, 'unchastity,' subtly reflecting the lack of unanimity among scholars about the precise meaning of *porneia*. With 'marital unfaithfulness' the translators of the New International Version have reverted to the older view that sexual misconduct is what Jesus had in mind. In fact, there are three main variants of the meaning of *porneia*, along with different interpretations of the whole sentence, 'anyone who divorces his wife ... and marries another woman commits adultery.'

According to one view, *porneia* does not refer to sexual misconduct at all, but to unlawful marriages as set out in Jewish law. These may be within forbidden degrees of relationship as listed in Leviticus 18, or between Jews and Gentiles as frequently forbidden in the Old Testament. In other words, divorce is allowed, indeed commanded, where a marriage should never have occurred in the first place. The exception clause is particularly appropriate to Matthew's Gospel, which was written for Jewish Christians, to show that Christ's new law of marriage did not overturn the detailed provisions of the Old Testament.

Support for this view is found in the conclusions reached in the

[1] See William A. Heth and Gordon J. Wenham, *Jesus and Divorce*, pp. 106–110.

Council of Jerusalem in Acts 15. There it is recorded how the early church was deeply divided on the question of circumcision of Gentile converts. Some Jewish Pharisee Christians were demanding it, while Paul, Barnabas and Peter insisted it struck at the heart of the gospel of grace through faith. In the end, the Council settled against the necessity of Gentile circumcision, but, for the sake of peace in the early Christian communities, recommended that Gentile converts should abstain from food polluted by idols, from *porneia*, from the meat of strangled animals and from blood (see Acts 15:1–21, particularly verse 20).

If *porneia* means 'sexual immorality' (NIV) then it is the odd one out in the list. All the others are ritualistic demands, and Gentile converts were surely required to turn from sexual immorality anyway. Since the recommendations of the Jerusalem Council were designed to reduce tension between Jewish and Gentile Christians, the requirement to abstain from *porneia* must, like the others, be ritualistic and not moral. Gentile Christians should avoid marrying within the forbidden degrees of the Jewish law, and they should avoid marrying Jewish Christians as well. Further support for this view is drawn from I Corinthians 5, where Paul demands the expulsion of a Christian who has married his stepmother (see I Cor 5:1,2; cf. Lev 18:8).

The unlawful marriages view is attractive, in that it removes any discrepancy between the teaching of Jesus in Matthew's Gospel, and in Mark's and Luke's. It demands that divorce should be understood in terms of annulment rather than separation and remarriage, and it therefore enjoys the support of the Roman Catholic Church which allows annulment but forbids divorce. On the other hand, many scholars feel that it restricts the meaning of *porneia* too narrowly. That is not to say that divorce (and remarriage) is not forbidden to those who are married illegally in the first place.

An alternative view regards *porneia* as sexual immorality during the betrothal period only. Since consent constituted marriage, a man should be allowed to divorce his wife before they came together if she was unfaithful to him. Matthew's account of the birth of Jesus is called to support this view. When Joseph discovered that Mary was expecting a child while she was pledged to be married to him, he had in mind to divorce her quietly rather than expose her to public disgrace (see Matt 1:18,19).

Again, this view is attractive because it also removes apparent contradiction between the Gospels. By her infidelity, the betrothed girl has broken her agreement to marry. Since the marriage is not consummated, the husband must be released from the contract and allowed to seek someone else. Indeed, it could be argued that he would cause his wife to commit adultery if he went ahead with the wedding, since, through her behaviour, she has become 'married' to someone else.

On the other hand, as with the unlawful marriages view, the betroth- al interpretation requires that *porneia* is given a very limited meaning, and scholars generally reject it on these grounds. Again, this is not to deny that when a couple are promised in marriage to each other and one behaves unfaithfully, that the other partner may be released from the engagement.

Yet a further approach understands *porneia* as describing consorting with a cult prostitute in a pagan temple. This view links Jesus' teaching with the 'Pauline privilege' of I Corinthians 7. According to Paul, a Christian is 'not bound' if an unbelieving partner leaves. According to the apostasy view, consorting with a cult prostitute constitutes leaving, and so releases the Christian partner from the marriage.

Not only does this view demand an even more particular under- standing of *porneia* than the other two; it also requires a highly speculative interpretation of I Corinthians 7:12–15. We shall examine the Pauline material in closer detail later; suffice to say the weight of evidence does not justify the conclusions drawn.

Apart from attempts to understand the meaning of the word *por- neia*, some scholars have attempted to explain Matthew's exception clause, by concentrating on the sentence as a whole. One such approach is to equate *porneia* with the 'something indecent' in Deuteronomy 24:1, and then to suggest that Jesus refused to comment on the meaning of the Deuteronomy phrase. This view would then translate Matthew 5:32 and 19:9 as follows:

> I say to you, however, that everyone who dismisses his wife — setting aside the matter of *porneia* — makes her become an adulteress; and whoever marries her who has been dis- missed, commits adultery.
> I say to you, however, that if anyone dismisses his wife — *porneia* is not involved — and marries another, he commits adultery; and whoever marries one who has been dismis- sed, commits adultery.[1]

This view is attractive because it concentrates on the meaning of the passage as a whole, rather than concentrating on one word. It upholds the essential truth that Jesus was teaching, that God's law of marriage established in the beginning can never be compromised or altered by later rules given when men's hearts were hard. It also harmonises the different Gospel accounts of Jesus' teaching on marriage. Matthew, with Jewish readers in mind, shows an understanding of their situation, without in any way altering the truth and absolute standards of Jesus' teaching. Yet for all its attraction it is doubtful if the view can be sus-

[1] See William A. Heth and Gordon J. Wenham, *Jesus and Divorce*, p. 181.

tained on grammatical grounds. The construction of the Greek words does not allow for this translation.[1]

One further explanation of the exception clauses in Matthew 5 and 19 is to regard them as additions, by the author, to the original teaching of Jesus more accurately reflected in Luke and Mark. By the time the *Gospel according to Matthew* was written, pastoral practice was already making the application of Jesus' teaching difficult, so the author added the exception clauses to allow divorce for *porneia*. This view reflects a particular approach to the whole of the New Testament, regarding its contents as late compositions which convey the teaching of the first century church, rather than the words of Jesus and the apostles themselves. Its main drawback, as we shall see, is that it does not reflect the teaching of the early church, which for centuries refused to allow divorcees to remarry.

Controversy continues to surround the meaning of Jesus' words, 'except for *porneia*', and their application in today's world. Before drawing our own conclusions, we pause to examine Paul's teaching on divorce, and the changing attitudes of the church down the ages.

The Pauline privilege

We cannot leave Jesus' teaching on divorce without looking briefly at Paul's application of it in I Corinthians 7. Basic to his position is his assertion, 'A wife must not separate from her husband. But if she does, she must remain unmarried or else be reconciled to her husband. And a husband must not divorce his wife' (I Cor 7:10,11). In this, he is totally consistent with Jesus' teaching in the Gospels. Indeed, he says the command is the Lord's and not his.

Then he deals with the practical problem of Christians who are married to unbelievers. If the unbelieving partner is willing, the marriage should continue. Both the unbelieving partner and the children will benefit. Indeed, they may find salvation themselves (see I Cor 7:12–14,16).

However, 'if an unbeliever leaves, let him do so. A believing man or woman is not bound in such circumstances; God has called us to live in peace' (I Cor 7:15). This provision is known as the 'Pauline privilege'. In the interests of peace, it allows a Christian to separate from an unbelieving partner when the latter insists on dissolving the marriage. But is that Christian then required to remain unmarried, as verse 11 directs, or does Paul's clause, 'not bound,' mean that he or she is free to marry again?

From this chapter we have learned that Moses, Jesus and Paul all recognise that because of our fallen human nature, we shall not always

[1] See William A. Heth and Gordon J. Wenham, *Jesus and Divorce*, p. 188.

attain to God's original intention of lifelong, faithful marriage. 'Something indecent,' may cause a rift which a husband and wife may find intolerable. Because our hearts are hard and we cannot love as we should, we may have to separate from each other. Immoral behaviour will always damage the exclusive relationship of married partners and may destroy it altogether. Where faith in Christ comes between husband and wife, mutually agreed separation may be the only way forward, and the Christian partner may have to recognise this.

In any event, we should not divorce each other easily. We must give ourselves time to be reconciled and try again. Like Hosea and Gomer we must be willing to forgive deeply hurtful and destructive behaviour in each other. But if, at the end of the day, we have to separate and divorce, may we then, as Christians, marry again, without destroying God's plan for our lives and disobeying Jesus' teaching? On this central, crucial issue Christians remain deeply divided.

CHAPTER 16

From Hermas to Augustine

IN their recent exhaustive study, *Jesus and Divorce*, William Heth and Gordon Wenham have argued that the only way to understand New Testament teaching on divorce correctly is to see how the early church understood it. Since the leaders of the early church still used Greek as their natural language, and since they were close in time to Jesus and the apostles, their understanding of the Gospels is likely to be far more accurate than ours. As a result they amass impressive evidence to show that, 'in the first five centuries all Greek writers and all Latin writers, except one, agree that remarriage following divorce for any reason is adulterous.'[1]

Typical is the position established by Hermas, a late first century or mid-second century writer, whose work was regarded as quasi-canonical by some of the later Fathers. In his *Mandate* he asks his heavenly guardian what a man should do if his wife persists in adultery. '"Let him send her away ... and let the husband remain single. But if after sending away his wife he marries another, he also commits adultery himself. ... This is the reason why you were commanded to remain single, whether husband or wife, because in such cases repentance is possible."'[2]

These themes, that a Christian may separate from his or her partner in the case of adultery, that divorced Christians who remarry commit adultery themselves, and that a divorced Christian should remain single to allow the other partner to repent are reiterated throughout the early centuries of the church's life. Irenaeus, Origen, Tertullian, John Chrysostom, Ambrose, Jerome and Augustine are all totally consistent, besides a host of lesser-known names. Only one writer, Ambrosiaster, of unknown identity save that he wrote commentaries on Paul's epistles in the second half of the fourth century, stands apart from this tradition. 'In allowing divorcees to remarry he was ... a stranger to the dominant Christian attitudes of the early Church.'[3]

[1] William A. Heth and Gordon J. Wenham, *Jesus and Divorce,* p. 22.
[2] Quoted in *ibid.,* p. 24.   [3] *ibid.,* p. 38.

Except for *porneia*

The clue to a correct understanding of Matthew 19, according to Heth and Wenham, lies in the way we apply the exception clause to its context. The clause only applies to the preceding clause, 'anyone who divorces his wife,' and not to the succeeding one, 'and marries another.' In other words, I may divorce my wife if she commits adultery, but if I marry again during her lifetime, I shall be guilty of adultery myself.

Under the Mosaic legislation adultery was a capital offence (Lev 20:10). Although this law was no longer enforced in Jesus' day, a Jew who discovered that his wife had committed adultery was required to divorce her. Jesus recognised this, with the exception clause, but then radically restated the nature of divorce by refusing to allow remarriage afterwards. Because the marriage bond established by God in the beginning is indelible, adultery cannot break it, neither can divorce. If a divorced person remarries, he commits adultery because he is still married to his first wife.

Any other interpretation of Matthew 19 makes Jesus side with the followers of Shammai in the ongoing dispute about the proper grounds for divorce. (Yet, when confronted with Pharisaic legalism, Jesus never came down on one side or the other, but always gave a radical answer drawn from a correct understanding of God's word.) It also makes his teaching inconsistent with the simpler and all-embracing statements recorded in Mark and Luke. Equally, it neutralises the force of Jesus' teaching in the Sermon on the Mount. If Jesus is saying there that we can divorce and remarry for adultery there is nothing new in his position. In fact he is saying far more than this. A man who divorces his wife causes her to commit adultery because he releases her to marry someone else. By the same token, he commits adultery himself if he marries a divorced woman, because she is still married to her first husband (see Matt 5:31,32).

If we apply the exception clause to remarriage as well as to divorce, certain other inconsistencies follow. If my wife commits adultery I may, apparently, divorce her and remarry without committing adultery myself. But if I divorce her for any other reason and remarry, then I am guilty of adultery. So divorce means 'with freedom to remarry' in one situation, while in another situation it means 'separation only.' It is hardly likely that the Greek word can carry this double meaning in the text as it stands.

More seriously, a woman who is divorced for adultery may remarry. What is allowed to her husband must be allowed to her also. But if she is divorced for any other reason she may not remarry, for the man marrying her will be guilty of adultery! The only consistent way to understand Matthew 19 is to recognise that Jesus limits divorce to separation. The divine law of marriage creates an indelible bond between husband and wife which no legal process can break. 'Therefore, what God has joined together, let man not separate.'

The eunuch saying

Understanding the exception clause as allowing divorce but not remarriage also makes sense of the disciples' objection to Jesus' reply to the Pharisees. Matthew tells us that the disciples were so appalled at Jesus' teaching that afterwards they said, 'If this is the situation between a husband and wife, it is better not to marry' (Matt 19:10). They would hardly have objected so strongly if Jesus had simply confirmed the view taken by Shammai, which allowed divorce and remarriage for adultery. No, they fully understood that in his reply (spoken, of course, in Aramaic and not Greek), Jesus allowed divorce but not remarriage. 'If that's the case then,' they rejoined, 'we're better off not getting married at all!'

In reply, Jesus gives the eunuch statement: '"Not everyone can accept this teaching, but only those to whom it has been given. For some are eunuchs because they were born that way; others were made that way by men; and others have renounced marriage because of the kingdom of heaven. The one who can accept this should accept it"' (Matt 19:11,12).

Commentators on Matthew's Gospel have frequently regarded this saying as unconnected with the earlier discussion with the Pharisees. They have understood it as an independent statement encouraging celibacy for the sake of the kingdom of heaven and have linked it with I Corinthians 7:32–25, where Paul defines the benefits of remaining single in order wholly to serve the Lord.

However, if Jesus' saying is kept in the context of his answer to the Pharisees, forbidding remarriage after divorce, those who have renounced marriage because of the kingdom of heaven are those who, having separated from their wives, are avoiding remarriage out of obedience to Christ. Significantly, both before and after the eunuch saying, Jesus insists that divine grace is needed to accept his teaching. We are naturally appalled at the prospect of renouncing marriage for the rest of our lives, particularly after our marriage has broken down. But if we have a proper regard for God's word, if we truly understand the nature of the marriage relationship, that it makes us and our partner one flesh, that neither adultery, nor divorce, nor anything else can end that relationship, and if we acknowledge the Lordship of Christ whose grace is sufficient to meet all our needs, then, with his help and in his strength, out of obedience to him, we shall be able to renounce marriage because of the kingdom of heaven.

This was the way the earliest Christians understood Jesus' teaching on marriage and divorce. In a world that steadily fell apart they established Christian standards of marriage and applied them to the whole of society. However, fifteen hundred years after the birth of Christ their understanding was challenged, with results that are with us to the present day.

CHAPTER 17

Erasmus and the Reformers

Erasmus and salvation

Desiderius Erasmus of Rotterdam was an Augustinian monk and priest who remained faithful to the Catholic Church until his death in 1536. Nevertheless, he made the Reformation inevitable; as his fellow monks would complain, he laid the egg which Luther hatched.

Erasmus was a humanist, not in the modern sense of the word meaning an atheist or agnostic who believes that man is capable of solving his problems without reference to God, but in the sense that in his thinking he started with man and his well-being and worked his way to God, rather than proceeding in the opposite direction. Along with many of his contemporaries he was also fascinated by the ancient world of Greece and Rome. He sought out classical manuscripts from monastic libraries where they had lain long forgotten, translated them, and believed it was possible to combine classical thought with Christian faith. In 1516 he published his own edition of the Greek New Testament, the first ever to be printed, and thus delivered later scholars from the inaccuracies of the Vulgate.

When Erasmus looked at the state of marriage at the turn of the sixteenth century he was deeply shocked. By making it into a technical sacrament, the Church had institutionalised it; by denying divorce it condemned hundreds of thousands of unhappily married couples to a lifetime of misery which, Erasmus believed, destroyed their hope of salvation. The church's procedure for annulment, with its 18 impediments to marriage, was grossly abused and without Scriptural warrant. Nor was marriage a sacrament since it had not been instituted by Christ.

For Erasmus, Christianity was a quality of life rather than the keeping of outward observances and the holding of doctrinal suppositions. He believed it should be possible to solve the ethical problem of unhappy marriage by finding a solution based on Scripture and centred on Christ. No ecclesiastical institution should be allowed to stand in the way of this objective. If unhappily married couples could be released from their misery and allowed to marry again, they could be saved. Charity must always guide our actions in seeking human salvation. Charity sometimes does what it legally should not do and is justified in doing so. The Church should always seek the salvation of those who suffer.

Erasmus found the solution to his problem of marriage and divorce by reversing the process of Scriptural understanding outlined in the previous chapter. Instead of starting with the statements of Jesus as recorded in Luke and Mark, and then harmonising the longer and more difficult passage in Matthew with them, he worked in the opposite direction. The statement in Matthew defined Jesus' position; Mark and Luke assumed the exception clause and should be understood accordingly.

Jesus obviously allowed divorce for adultery since adultery is so destructive of the marriage bond. If a man were not allowed to divorce his wife he might kill her. Once divorced it would be cruel to refuse remarriage. Divorce in the New Testament always assumed remarriage. Jesus never demanded celibacy of his followers, least of all those who had already been married, nor did he demand that his followers behave contrary to nature.

Erasmus was genuinely motivated by a deep desire to promote human happiness and salvation among married people. In his teaching he departed from fifteen hundred years of consistent Christian teaching on marriage and divorce. Nevertheless, he was eagerly followed by the Reformers who broke away from the church to which Erasmus remained faithful. In view of their insistence that in so doing they were returning to the faith of the New Testament and the Fathers, it is interesting to ask why.

Luther and divorce

Luther's initial protest at abuse within the Catholic Church quickly turned, as we have seen, to total rejection of all that Rome stood for in terms of mediaeval doctrine and practice. Erasmus' position on marriage, as a learned Catholic scholar, obviously had an immediate appeal and, no doubt, helps to explain Luther's and the other Reformers' uncritical support. If marriage was not a sacrament, neither was it indissoluble, nor should it be denied to ministers of God's word. If marriage was not a sacrament, matrimonial jurisdiction should lie with the state rather than with the church. In the same way the state should regulate and control divorce. From being a doctrinal impossibility divorce becomes more a matter of pastoral concern and practice.

Following Erasmus' interpretation of Matthew 19 and comparing it with I Corinthians 7, Luther at first insisted that divorce should only be allowed for adultery and desertion. He justified this by introducing the idea of 'legal fiction.' Because the Old Testament prescribed death for adulterers (see Lev 20:10), a married person who was unfaithful should be regarded as legally dead. Therefore, by their adultery they ended the marriage bond, and, because they were 'dead,' they released their partner to marry again. Luther extended this principle to desertion. Through deserting a spouse, a partner similarly became as dead, and thus released the spouse to marry again.

Together with the idea of legal fiction, Luther also introduced the concept of the innocent party. Only the innocent party should be allowed to divorce, and then, only after they had proved the other guilty of a matrimonial offence. These ideas would duly pass into divorce law, and would involve divorcees in costly law suits in order to secure release from their marriages. They introduced an ethical dimension into an area of intimate human relationship; who is innocent and who is guilty when a marriage breaks down? They resulted in a great deal of hypocrisy as couples who decided on divorce agreed to provide sufficient evidence to allow a suit to be filed.

Luther himself became aware of some of these problems. Once he had opened the Pandora's box of divorce and allowed it for some reasons, he found, like the Pharisees of old, that he needed to add others too. Impotence, and refusal to render conjugal duty, were added to the list. Others would later include cruelty as well. Although he would have staunchly denied it, today's crisis of easy divorce on demand has its roots in the Reformation turmoil of the sixteenth century.

Luther's position on divorce was largely followed by Calvin, Beza and the English Reformers, though Canon 107 of the Church of England, published in 1603 required that separated partners 'shall live "chastely and continently," neither shall they, during each other's life, contract matrimony with any other person.'[1]

On the other hand the Westminster Confession of 1648, which defined the course of subsequent Protestant belief and practice, allowed divorce for adultery or fornication during the betrothal period. 'In the case of adultery after marriage, it is lawful for the innocent party to sue out a divorce (Matt 5:32), and after the divorce to marry another, as if the offending party were dead (Matt 19:9; Rom 7:2,3).' Adultery and desertion were the only proper grounds for divorce, and then, only after 'a public and orderly course of proceedings.'[2]

So Protestant toleration of divorce was established. For long it remained the preserve of the rich and was so rare as to be scarcely noticed. Today it has become a tidal wave, undermining the historic Christian position of lifelong, faithful marriage, and threatening the very future stability of society itself.

[1] Quoted in William A. Heth and Gordon J. Wenham, *Jesus and Divorce*, p. 82.
[2] Quoted in *ibid.*, p. 83.

CHAPTER 18

Jesus and Sinners

GUESTS had gathered for an exclusive dinner-party. Polite talk and restrained laughter filled the room, mingling with the clink of glasses and the aroma of exotic food. Yet one of the guests was out of place. Beneath their veneer of good manners and forced bonhomie the others eyed him cautiously, careful to restrain their conviviality lest they should be seen to warm too closely to the wandering carpenter from Galilee who fearlessly challenged their most cherished ideals. Simon the host had invited him out of self-righteous condescension. He wanted to appear liberal and tolerant among his Pharisaic colleagues; perhaps in such exalted company he could reduce Jesus to size.

As the party reclined on low couches around the table, heavily-laden with tempting food and wine, an uninvited girl entered the room sending a muffled gasp of astonishment and embarrassment from one guest to another. They all knew her, the village prostitute. Had some of them known her intimately, stealing at dead of night for her embrace, to escape from the stifling restrictions of their religious observance? In the small, gossiping village where everyone knew everyone else, how had she entered on her life of shame? Had she once been married, like all the other girls, and then divorced when her infidelity was discovered? We are not told, but in the tightly-knit community where girls were kept from men until their fathers approved their betrothal, it is hard to imagine any other way. Why had she come? To create a scene; to expose a lover; to demand back-payment for services given?

Loosening her hair till it fell to her waist she dropped to her knees behind the Galilaean stranger. Bursting into tears, she began to smother his feet with her kisses. Breaking open a precious alabaster jar of expensive perfume, she poured it liberally from his ankles to his toes until the smell filled the room. All the while she continued to weep and to kiss, and then to dry the tear-stained, perfumed feet with her tresses. None of the onlookers had ever felt so uncomfortable. So Jesus was her latest *amour*! They might have known! No wonder he attacked their religious conventions! He had to salve his conscience somehow. 'If this man were a prophet, he would know who is touching him and what kind of woman she is — that she is a sinner' (Luke 7:39).

Replying to Simon's unspoken thoughts, Jesus told the story of the two debtors, one who owed 500 denarii and the other 50. When neither could repay, the creditor cancelled the debts. 'Which will love him the more?' he asked. 'The one who had the bigger debt cancelled,' Simon replied. 'That's right,' said Jesus. 'When I came here, you gave me no water to wash my feet, nor did you greet me with a kiss. But this woman has washed my feet with her tears, dried them with her hair, and has never stopped kissing me from the moment she entered. In place of your oil she has poured her perfume. Therefore, I tell you, because she loves me so much, her many sins are forgiven.' Then, turning to the woman, Jesus declared, 'Your sins are forgiven, your faith has saved you; go in peace' (see Luke 7:38–50).

Jesus' response to the woman in Simon's house was typical of his attitude to sinners. An insertion into John's Gospel, nonetheless generally regarded as authentic, describes his confrontation with a woman caught in the act of adultery. "Moses says she should be stoned! What do you say?" gloated the exultant Pharisees. Again, he exposed their hypocrisy; after all, where was the man with whom she had been found? Was he not guilty, too? Writing in the dust with his finger, Jesus calmly declared, "Let him who is without sin cast the first stone." One by one they slunk away until Jesus and the woman were left alone. "Where are they?" he asked. "Has no-one condemned you?" "No-one sir," she said. "Then neither do I condemn you," Jesus declared. "Go now and leave your life of sin" (see John 8:1–11). To be caught in adultery she must have been married. If she was not to be stoned, she must certainly be divorced. If she was divorced, and forgiven, could she remarry?

On another occasion, Jesus rested by a Samaritan well while his disciples went to the nearby town to buy food. Breaking all social and racial convention he struck up a conversation with a Samaritan woman who came alone to the well in the heat of the day. He offered her living water which would well up within and bring eternal life, and when she asked for his gift he told her, "Go, call your husband and come back." "I have no husband," she replied. Jesus said to her, "You are right when you say you have no husband. The fact is, you have had five husbands, and the man you now have is not your husband." Divorced and divorced, again and again until she entered into a relationship which fell short of marriage, this woman still had a 'husband'. And Jesus accepted her as she was. He offered her the water of life and declared himself the Messiah.

If we are to find a way through the tortuous arguments which surround the meaning of Jesus' words in the Gospels about marriage and divorce, and if we are to apply his teaching with integrity and compassion in the ethical morass of today's permissive society, I believe we have to balance his behaviour towards sinners against his discussions with the Pharisees and with his disciples. Only so shall we come to a rounded understanding of his will for our lives, whether married or unmarried, whether faithful or failing in our obedience to his commands.

When Jesus disputed with the Pharisees he was confronted by people who, perhaps with the very best of intentions, had unknowingly and unwittingly concentrated on some of the details of God's law to the point where they had forgotten and even denied its eternal principles. In arguing for and against easy divorce, the followers of Shammai and Hillel were neglecting the eternal principles, laid down in the beginning, on which true marriage is built. In their self-righteous certainty that they had all the answers, they had become hypocrites, relying on their own goodness instead of on God's mercy. So with them, Jesus was uncompromising. Marriage is a lifelong union between a man and a woman who are made in the image of God. We may not look for reasons to divorce each other and marry someone else, even when our partner fails to love us as he or she should, for marital breakdown always opens the door to adultery.

But when Jesus met sinners who had failed to obey God's law and knew it, he was always forgiving. He knew how they felt, for he was made sin for us (see II Cor 5:21). He knew that more often than not they were more sinned against than sinning, deeply ashamed at their behaviour, and at the same time embittered towards those who had hurt them. So he called them to repentance. He offered them new life, living water after which they would never again thirst (John 4:14). And he told them to go in peace, and leave their life of sin.

In *Jesus and Divorce*, Heth and Wenham have done a great service in exposing the inconsistencies in the Erasmian, and therefore the Protestant, interpretation of the divorce passages in the Synoptic Gospels. If we are Protestant, they have rightly urged us to reconsider our position, to re-examine the texts in the light of modern scholarship, and against the background of the way they were understood by the early church. But I believe their treatment is defective in this vital respect; they ignore the way Jesus responded to sinners.

Because of the fallibility of human nature, God's people have always had to recognise and deal with sexual and marital failure. In the Old Testament we have the Deuteronomic legislation, and in the inter-testamental period the dispute betwen Shammai and Hillel. And the early church too, for all the apprent inflexibility of its teaching, still had to recognise and allow divorce. Heth and Wenham themselves admit that Basil of Caesarea and Origen permitted remarriage after divorce, although it was contrary to the Scriptures, as a means of avoiding greater evils. And they quote a certain Pollentius who invented the legal fiction that an adulterous partner was 'as dead', more than a thousand years before it was resurrected by Martin Luther.[1]

In his attempts to solve an ethical problem, based on Scripture and centred in Christ, Erasmus was essentially right. Unfortunately, he concentrated exclusively in forcing a meaning out of Christ's words, 'except for *porneia*' which the immediate context would not bear, and which has caused confusion ever since among those who have tried to follow his line. A more constructive way is to consider in tandem the twin aspects of Jesus' ministry: his teaching and his attitude to sinners. This may not always produce neat and tidy solutions, but, conscious of the law of Christ, and dependent on the Spirit of Christ, we may then hope to discern the mind of Christ in the differing situations we face.

[1] William A. Heth and Gordon J. Wenham, *Jesus and Divorce*, p. 42f.

CHAPTER 19

The Plight of the Divorced

BILL and June courted each other for five years. They saved hard, bought a house and furnished it. And one day, with great joy, in front of their families and friends, they were married in the Baptist church where June had grown up. Three months later, Bill decided he had had enough of June. He simply left, just walked out, and headed down a slippery slope of immorality and promiscuity. He made it clear he wanted nothing more to do with June. After he had gone, she discovered she was expecting his child.

Are we really to believe that Jesus, the Saviour of love and forgiveness, denies to June any opportunity to marry again, as long as Bill is alive? Does Jesus, who by his death on the cross deals with the past with all its failure, tell June that her marriage is indissoluble, and therefore, if she marries another, she is guilty of adultery?

Naturally, June was utterly devastated by the failure of her brief marriage. She did not know where to turn. But her parents, who, incidentally, had always had their doubts about Bill, were marvellous. They took her back home, helped her through all the legal tangles that followed, welcomed her child with open arms, and did all they could to support them both in the early months and years of the infant's life. And, because June was a warm-hearted girl with a great capacity for love, in time, she met and fell in love with Dave. From the start, she told him everything about Bill. Undaunted, he asked her to marry him and, despite her previous disappointment, she found the courage to say 'Yes.' After the marriage, Dave adopted Bill's child as his own and their life together was happy and fulfilled. Are June and Dave living in sin? Did Dave commit adultery when he married June? Has their church compromised the teaching of Jesus and the apostles by celebrating their wedding, and welcoming them into its life and fellowship?

Sybil's marriage never really worked. Her husband was selfish and inconsiderate. Nevertheless, Sybil believed in Christ and believed in marriage. Children were born and a family was raised. When, after 20 years of growing tension, Sybil's husband left for another woman, she was stricken with guilt at her 'failure'. The children grew up and moved away from home. Sybil herself made a new start in another area of the town. All contact between herself and her former husband was lost. Nevertheless, because she believed in marriage, Sybil never considered marrying again while her husband was alive.

But across the road lived Andrew, a single man in middle life. Slowly, from casual greetings in the street, a friendship began to grow between him and Sybil. Soon he was giving her lifts in his car to church, and staying to join in the services. Through the worship and listening to the minister's preaching he came to a living faith in Christ. And one day, he overcame his shyness and diffidence, and asked Sybil to marry him. With the failure of her first marriage now far behind her, Sybil accepted his proposal. Are she and Andrew also living in sin? Has their church too, condoned their adultery by conducting their wedding and embracing them in its life?

Indissoluble or indelible?

By recalling us to the clear and undiluted teaching of Jesus and the apostles, Heth and Wenham have eloquently restated the true ethic of marriage. Christians should not divorce their husbands and wives. If their life together becomes intolerable, through infidelity, or violence or any other cause, they may separate, but should then refrain from remarriage, to allow for repentance and reconciliation. But what of the partner who believes in marriage, who does all they can to make it work, and who is still divorced, deserted and left alone while their former partner goes and marries someone else? According to Deuteronomy 24, they should never remarry their original partner, even if that partner's second marriage breaks down and the partner wants them back! Surely then, a second marriage must release the original spouse from the obligations of the first! The 'legal fiction' is not fiction, but fact. By marrying again, a spouse has killed a former marriage. Therefore, the other spouse must be free to remarry as well.

In I Corinthians 7, Paul contrasts the broken Christian marriage with the mixed marriage which fails. A Christian wife must not separate from her husband. But if she does, she must remain unmarried or else be reconciled. And a husband must not divorce his wife (see verses 10,11). Then, as now, people reacted against living single lives once they had been married. If they separated, they expected to marry someone else. 'No' says Paul to the Corinthians, 'you Christians must be different. If you have to separate, remain unmarried, or else resume your marriage.'

If, however, an unbeliever deserts a Christian partner, the situation is different. Since the unbeliever will almost certainly marry someone else, "a believing man or woman is not bound in such circumstances" (see verse 15). Not bound to what? They cannot be bound to the obligations of the original marriage, since by deserting them and marrying again the former partner destroyed all hope of repentance and reconciliation. As a Jew and a Pharisee, Paul would have been as aware of Deuteronomy 24 as we are, and must have written to the Corinthians with it in mind. Surely, we must understand "bound" in verse 15, where the unbeliever has deserted, in the same sense as "bound" in verse 39, where Paul declares, "A woman is bound to her husband as long as he lives. But if her husband dies, she is free to marry anyone she wishes, but he must belong to the Lord." The same rule must apply to the deserted, as to the widowed believer.

While we do not recommend Christians to divorce their partners, the same rule must similarly apply when a husband or wife has taken the initiative and the first partner has married again. The second marriage kills the first and thereby releases the divorced 'survivor' to marry someone else. This in no sense undermines the force of Jesus' teaching in the Gospels about remarriage and adultery; it is the inevitable result of viewing Scripture as a whole rather than defining our doctrine and practice from individual parts of it viewed in isolation from each other. We shall be suggesting in a later chapter that many of our modern problems derive from the way in which most people register marital breakdown by filing for divorce rather than judicial separation. If we use the latter option when life becomes impossible, we leave the door open for reconciliation, however impossible this may seem at the time, and we face the challenge of becoming eunuchs for the kingdom of heaven in accordance with Matthew 19.

The whole divorce and remarriage problem really stems from the view that marriage is indissoluble.

Yet, in Chapter 5, we showed that this is closely connected with the idea that marriage is a technical sacrament, an effective sign of God's grace whereby we are caught up into Christ's redemptive work in the world. But this is a mediaeval view of marriage, the product of scholastic speculation in the thirteenth century. Erasmus and the Reformers rightly rejected it because they could not find it in the New Testament. Instead of indissoluble, we prefer the word, indelible, to describe the permanent effect marriage always has on us. Once we have been joined to another and have become one flesh with them we are never the same again. This is as true of the widow as of the divorcee. We allow a widow to come as a married person to a second marriage, so why not a divorcee whose marriage has broken down and can never be repaired? A constant tendency in the Catholic tradition has been to forbid remarriage to the widowed. If marriage is indissoluble, this is not surprising.

Marriage is not indissoluble. Death, quite clearly dissolves it. So do divorce and remarriage if, as a result, the original partners are forbidden to marry each other again (see Deut 24:1–4). Persistent selfishness and cruelty may also dissolve a marriage. Muriel and George married over 40 years ago. They met, as respectable couples often did in those days, walking sedately in the park with friends on summer evenings. From the start, it quickly became clear that they were not going to get on. Yet somehow, they managed to conceive, bear a child and bring him up. All the while, their quarrels became more bitter and violent. Now in their eighties, they still fight as fiercely as ever. They rake up incidents from years long gone. Muriel accuses George of infidelity of which he has never been guilty. Driven to exasperation by her constant nagging, George busies himself in the garden whenever he can, or puts himself into a rest home from time to time for some peace and quiet. For years they have slept in separate rooms.

Muriel and George have been legally and physically married. To the rest of the world they are still married. But their marriage is dead, and has been for decades. Hardened by a lifetime of misery, each blames and accuses the other. All attempts, and there have been many, by family, friends and Christian ministry to bring reconciliation and repair have failed. George says he should have left Muriel when their son grew up and married. He is right. When marriages die, their death should be recognised.

Divorce, the unforgivable sin?

If, as Christians, we refuse to allow all divorced people to remarry on condemnation of adultery, we end up making divorce the unforgivable sin. Guilt, blame and shame are the inevitable results of divorce, not least among those who have tried the hardest to save their failing marriages. Then to be condemned for the rest of their lives to celibacy, and denied the chance to remarry on pain of adultery can only add to their guilt, and is contrary to the compassion of Christ. Furthermore, it makes hypocrites of us all, for it allows us to tolerate, and then forgive, the most horrendous sexual and quasi-marital misdemeanours before marriage, but not a mistaken marriage. For that, apparently, there can be no forgiveness. By living celibate, the divorced person must bear the shame for the rest of his own or his partner's life.

In *Meant to Last*, Paul Steel and Charles Ryrie tell the story of Wanda, who, at 16, ran away from home to marry Fred, four years her senior. Drugs, liquor, violence, sadism and indescribable degradation followed. When Fred finally left her for another girl, Wanda returned home and turned to Christ. Transformed, she sought reconciliation with her wayward husband, but failed to prevent him from divorcing her and marrying his new partner. Now, according to the authors, after careful instruction in the Scriptures, Wanda is committed in obedience to Christ, to avoiding remarriage, as long as Fred is alive.[1]

---

[1] Paul E. Steele and Charles C. Ryrie, *Meant to Last,* pp. 119–121.

The only thing wrong with this story is Wanda's marriage. Had she simply run away from home and lived with Fred for five years there would be no bar to her getting married. Her marriage hardly qualified anyway: 'a late night session with a justice of the peace,' is how the authors describe it. We are creating a new Pharisaism here. I may live with a partner for ten years or more, buy a house and raise a family together. To all intents and purposes we become married people. Then we may separate and I am able to marry someone else. But if I have gone through a marriage ceremony, however foolish and ill-advised, I may never marry again while my partner is alive.

Heth and Wenham believe that couples who have remarried after divorce, 'should see that your present marriage is now God's will for you.'[1] Really! They may be right. God does accept us as we are and give us his new life. But there is something decidedly odd about a situation wherein, at ten o'clock in the morning I can step outside the will of God by marrying a divorcee, or by marrying again after I have been divorced, and at eleven o'clock, when the ceremony is over, I can be back in the centre of God's will! Again, we are falling into the trap of the Pharisees who tried to legislate for every human situation. The more we try, the more foolish we become.

None of this debate is designed to dilute the seriousness of divorce or to undermine the teaching of our Lord. God hates divorce (see Mal 2:16). If we divorce and remarry we commit adultery. And if we marry someone who is divorced we commit adultery also, for they have already been joined to their former spouse. Nevertheless, we have to remember that those hard sayings of Jesus were spoken to men who were trying to trap him, and who, in their self-righteous religiosity were trying to find ways round the ultimate standards of God's law. A divorced woman was not an automatic alternative for a Pharisee who was fed up with his wife and wanted a change. Nor did marriage neutralise an affair which had occasioned the divorce in the first place.

But divorced people can be forgiven. And if because of remarriage, or desertion, or alcoholism or persistent cruelty or whatever, there is no hope of ever rebuilding the original marriage, then divorced people must be free to marry again. "Divorce is a sin," said a divorcee recently, "and it was only when I understood that, and accepted God's forgiveness for my part in the failure of my first marriage, that I realised I could be free to marry again."

Divorced and remarried people often need forgiveness too. In contrast to their story of Wanda, Steel and Ryrie describe Homer and Mary, both of whom had been married before and whose union was heading for disaster like their first marriages. When Homer was finally persuaded to confess to Mary his sin in encouraging her to marry him,

[1] William A. Heth and Gordon J. Wenham, *Jesus and Divorce*, p. 200.

117

a divorced man, she confessed her guilt too, and their marriage was saved.[1]

There is forgiveness with Christ for every sin, including the sin of divorce. When he forgives, he washes clean and makes us new. If he can wash away my fornication and cleanse me to marry someone else, he can wash away the failure of my marriage as well. He can heal my bitterness at the behaviour of my former husband or wife. He can reach the inner wounds in my character which make me impossible to live with, and he can equip me to marry again and to display in my love for another, his love for his church. Let us beware, lest we deny to the divorced that which many of them need most, the certainty of Christ's love and forgiveness, the assurance of his restoring power to pick up the pieces of their shattered lives and begin again, and the opportunity to display his redeeming work in their lives in a second union which, unlike their first, reflects his saving love for his Church.

[1] Paul E. Steele and Charles C. Ryrie, *Meant to Last*, p. 139f.

CHAPTER 20

Divorce, Remarriage, and the Church

ONE of the great social evils of our day is not divorce in general, but divorce for the specific purpose of marrying someone else. If we could not marry again for five years after a divorce, there would be many more reconciliations than currently occur. Thousands of divorced people regret ending their marriages and wish they could return to their former partners. Yet, time and again, their wish is denied, simply because their partner has already married again. Remarriage, rather than divorce itself, is often the main cause of anguish suffered by the partner who is left, as well as by the children, who often feel personally guilty and to blame for the breakdown of their parents' marriage. Access and maintenance arrangements can sustain bitterness for years, particularly when one partner has married again.

Can we then, as Christians, ever encourage divorced people to marry again while their married prtner is alive, and can we assure them of Christ's blessing by conducting a subsequent wedding within the fellowship of the church? In the previous chapter we suggested that, if we consider the teaching of Christ on divorce in tandem with the compassion of Christ towards sinners and those who have failed, then we can not only assure divorced people of God's forgiveness, but, in recognising that their marriages have died, release them to marry again.

We cannot allow divorce and remarriage on demand. This is the way to moral anarchy and human heartbreak on a horrendous scale. When then can we encourage divorced people to enter a subsequent marriage? Are there principles which can guide us? What follows is an attempt to outline the kind of questions we should ask before we consent to the marriage of divorced people. The rules suggested are not intended to be applied in a hard and fast way. Prayer and counselling will need to accompany their use. Situations alter cases. More than anything, recognition of past failure and repentance for past sin should be displayed by the divorced people concerned. Some degree of assurance that this marriage can succeed where the previous one failed, and a willingness to accept after-care when further difficulties come should also be indicated.

Guidelines for remarriage

'A woman is bound to her husband as long as he lives. But if her husband dies, she is free to marry anyone she wishes, but he must belong to the Lord' (I Cor 7:39). If Paul gave that advice to widows, how much more important is it for divorced people to belong to the Lord before they marry again. Marriage, as we have seen, is a relationship with a spiritual dimension. Therefore, those who cultivate their relationship with Christ are more likely to live faithfully and lovingly together than those who live purely for themselves.

In this book we have deliberately avoided discussing whether or not we can offer Christian marriage in church to people who are not practising Christians. But where divorced people are concerned we should be very careful before we offer them Christian marriage, particularly if they show no inclination to live in a Christian way before or after they marry.

For many, of course, the trauma of divorce brings them to Christ and the joy or discovering him helps to heal the wounds caused by the breakdown of their marriage. Then they sometimes facilely imagine that, if they only marry a Christian, all will be well. So they fall for the first Christian who comes along and forget that the wounds in their personality, which contributed to the breakdown of their first marriage, will create tension in a second marriage unless they are finally healed.

Three out of ten first marriages currently end in divorce. Four to five out of ten second and subsequent marriages end the same way. Therefore the success rate among remarrying people is lower than among those who are marrying for the first time. This means that people who are contemplating marrying again after divorce should only do so after the most careful thought. If marriage first time round 'must not be undertaken carelessly, lightly or selfishly,' then a reverent, responsible and serious approach second time round is even more important.[1]

Christian pastors can refuse to remarry people whose first partners, although divorced, have not married again. Although all hope of reconciliation may seem to have passed, nevertheless the grace of God can be active in seemingly hopeless situations. As long as there is a chance, however slight, that the divorced couple might settle their differences and resume their marriages, we must discourage either of them from marrying someone else. This is fully in line with Paul's teaching in I Corinthians 7:10,11. An exception to this rule may be allowed where, for instance, a divorced couple have lost all contact with each other for several years and one may not be sure whether the other has remarried or not. Perhaps a divorced partner has emigrated

---

[1] *The Alternative Service Book 1980, The Marriage Service,* para. 6.

and is unlikely, therefore, ever to return. But, generally speaking, remarriage by one partner while the divorced partner has not married again should be discouraged by the Christian church.

Then, we can refuse to remarry people where one partner in the new relationship was instrumental in the breakdown of the first marriage. This quite clearly falls under the ban of adultery set out by Jesus in the Gospels. Remarriage after an affair is wrong, however unreasonable the original partner may apparently have been. In any event, evidence shows it is unlikely to succeed. Those who are unfaithful to one spouse are less likely to remain faithful to another. When the excitement of the chase and the illicit affair are ended and the second marriage begins to pall, they will then begin again to look round for someone else.

Rather more controversially, we should be very careful before we encourage people to remarry where access and maintenance arrangements for children of the previous marriage are still in force. When children are seeing an estranged parent regularly and mothers are receiving alimony for those children, the former marriage has not finally died. Being divorced is 'just another way of being married. You may not be husband and wife any more, but you will both go on being parents till the day you die.'[1]

The presence of children from a former marriage forms one of the biggest obstacles to the establishment of a successful second marriage. Sometimes they happily adjust to a step-parent, but often they bitterly resent his or her arrival. Remarried people are rarely prepared for the reaction of their children to their union. They fondly imagine that all will settle down into a nice, new, happy family and are bemused and bewildered when this does not happen.

Equally, divorced husbands and wives often resent their partners remarrying. Something deep inside tells them they still belong to each other. If they are still seeing their children on a regular basis, they can convey their feelings through them, sometimes with disturbing and distressing results. Parents vie for their children's affection and loyalty while at the same time using them to prolong the bitterness surrounding their marital breakdown. Bring a step-parent into this equation and the children are caught, even more haplessly, in the middle of a triangular battle.

Divorce is still an expensive business. Many are unprepared for the cost in alimony of maintaining a former wife and family. If the wife remarries, the husband will naturally resent the continuing cost of paying for his children. He may complain that it prevents him from marrying again himself, since he cannot afford to support two households. If the wife and her new husband are poor and need the payments, that demonstrates that the first marriage has not finally died, since the wife

[1] Gay Search, *How to Survive Divorce, Living Magazine,* May 1983, p. 6.

is still dependent on her original husband.

It may seem hard to tell a single parent, struggling to bring up two or three children on a limited income, to wait until the children have grown up before marrying again, but that is often the best advice. Widowed parents with young families are often willing to make a similar sacrifice, so why not divorced ones? Sometimes, if children are very small, or when a prospective step-parent has taken time to build a relationship with them, remarriage may be in order. But if the children continue to relate to a natural, estranged parent, then the newly-married couple must recognise that this will bring tension and will be an intrusion on their marriage with which they will have to cope, perhaps for many years to come.

Divorce is one of the deepest traumas through which human beings may have to pass, often exceeding bereavement in the grief and distress it arouses. That grief must be healed before any subsequent marriage can succeed. Associated guilt must be forgiven. Bitterness and resentment must be buried. The process takes time. One doctor advised a divorced woman, whose husband had left her with a young family, not to contemplate marrying again for at least five years. Wisely, she heeded his advice, and although she developed a friendship with another man during that period, she stopped short of sleeping with him and marrying him.

At the end of the day, the local Christian community must decide whether or not the church can give Christ's blessing to the subsequent marriage of someone who has been divorced; not the vicar, nor the minister, but the community. It must decide, not on the basis of emotions and feelings towards the people involved, nor on their position or social standing, but prayerfully, carefully, with due regard to biblical teaching, and with the best interests of all concerned. We shall outline a possible process which churches might adopt in a later chapter. Once an affirmative decision is taken, then the church must be committed to the continuing support of the newly-married couple. They will need all the help they can receive. But, with God's help, they can succeed where they failed before and can demonstrate Christ's redeeming love in the rebuilding of their lives together.

Blessing or Christian marriage?

After the advent of civil weddings in Western countries in the nineteenth century, Christian ministers began to be approached by married couples seeking God's blessing on their civil vows. Often, though not always, these were divorced people who had remarried. To accede to their requests, services of Blessing of a Civil Wedding, or Reaffirmation of Marriage Vows, were produced. In the eyes of many Christians, they allowed the church to maintain its high standard of lifelong marriage, while at the same time meeting the pastoral needs of people whose marriages had failed, yet who still wanted to enjoy the comfort and fellowship of the Church. Often, these services were scarcely distinguishable from marriage services themselves. Sometimes, couples would hurry from registry office to church, dressed in all their finery, for a service of hymns, ceremonial and prayers which cocked a snook at the church's insistence that married people could not remarry during the lifetime of their partners without committing adultery.

Even today, many leading Christians still regard these services as a practical solution to the problem of remarriage after divorce, and are urging their use for all couples who request them. By providing a service which is almost marriage, the church, they argue, is nonetheless preserving Christian marriage for those who live faithfully together until death takes them away.

Others, however, are less sure. If the church can offer Christ's blessing on a civil wedding, why can it not marry the couple properly in the first place? After a service of blessing or reaffirmation of vows, are the couple truly married in God's sight, or, if they are divorced, are they living in adultery? If they are living in adultery, why are they welcomed into the fellowship of the church? In any event, do not the same guidelines which apply to the remarriage of divorcees apply equally to those who request a service of blessing?

'Consider the organist and his wife. They are happily married until, one day, a tenor joins the choir. A handsome man with a fine voice, he and the organist's wife have an affair. There is a divorce and a marriage. The tenor and former wife of the organist ask for a service of blessing. Even if the vicar was foolish enough to agree, it is doubtful whether the organist would be willing to play.'[1]

In the face of mounting pressure to remarry divorcees, some Christians are retreating by denying remarriage and services of blessing to all who have been married previously and who have a partner who is still alive. We have argued that this can be cruel and incompatible with the compassion of Christ. Where a couple had a civil wedding, say, because they were not Christians, and then later believe in Christ, reaffirmation of their vows before a Christian minister and their friends can be a moving expression of their new-found faith. But for the divorced, such services are no solution. Either we can, or we cannot, assure them of Christ's blessing on their marriage. If we can, can we offer them a marriage service which does not compromise Christian standards of lifelong marriage?

The Orthodox Churches of the East hold a strongly sacramental view of marriage, not in the technical sense of mediaeval Catholicism,

---

[1] Philip Crowe, *The Remarriage Dilemma, Church Times,* 4 January 1985.

but in the sense that natural marriage has been transformed into an antitype of the Kingdom of Heaven. They place crowns on the bridegroom and bride as signs that their marriage will be a witness to the Kingdom, a service of Christ in the world, and a special vocation within the Church.

Therefore, the Orthodox Churches insist that marriage is indissoluble, yet at the same time they recognise it is being dissolved all the time by sin and ignorance, passion and selfishness, lack of both faith and love. They acknowledge divorce while avoiding deciding on it. And, in compassion, these Churches allow the innocent party to marry again. But marriage services for the divorced are different from those for couples who marry for the first time. Their theme is penitential. They emphasise the need for intercession and love. Nothing of the glory and joy of the first union, which has been broken, remains.[1]

Whether we accept the sacramental theology of Orthodoxy or not, its practical solution to the problem of remarriage after divorce is admirable. It frankly recognises what has gone before. It openly seeks God's forgiveness for the failure and breakdown of the first union. And it requests his special grace for those who are bravely trying again, recognising that only with his help can they display his love for each other.

Is there not a lesson for us here? We avoid the hypocrisy of services of blessing by providing a full marriage service. Yet, through open confession we acknowledge what has gone before, through the ministry of the Word we reaffirm Christian standards of marriage, and through appropriate prayers we commend the newly-remarried couple to God's special care and blessing.

Divorced and remarried people in the Church

Whatever solution we find to the problems of remarriage after divorce, we shall still be faced with those who have remarried contrary to Christ's commands, and later, wish to be received into the fellowship of the church. The early Christians admitted them to deepening levels of church life after prolonged probation. In the fourth century, Basil of Caesarea decreed: 'Whoever has committed adultery will be excluded from the sacraments for fifteen years: he must weep for four years [outside the door of the church during the service], then he must listen for five years [in the vestibule], be prostrated [among the catechumens] for four years and then stand upright [among the full congregation] for two years without receiving communion.' Is such draconian discipline

---

[1] For a fuller discussion of the Orthodox understanding of marriage see Alexander Schmemann, *The Theological Tradition of the East,* in ed. W. Bassett *The Bond of Marriage.*

really necessary? More seriously, does it reflect the forgiving love of Christ?

On his missionary journeys the apostle Paul seems to have had little hesitation in admitting heinous sinners to the life of the church and in appointing them to positions of leadership within it once they had confessed Christ in baptism and had received the Holy Spirit. Is there anything so special about divorced and remarried converts to warrant us treating them any differently from others who believe in Jesus? To be sure, we may need to help them to repent of their sin in breaking off their original marriages in the first place. They may well be full of guilt anyway and may need the assurance, more than anything else, that God loves and receives them as they are. If their access and maintenance arrangements are in disarray, they may need practical help at this level too. But just as Jesus accepted the Samaritan woman as she was, with her live-in lover after being married and divorced by five husbands, so we must assure divorced and remarried people today, that he offers them the living water of life as well. They must be welcomed into the church's life, admitted to its sacraments and encouraged to exercise their gifts like everyone else.

When divorced and remarried people come as Christians, seeking to join a particular congregation, more caution may be required. Have they left an estranged partner in another congregation, angry and hurt at their action? Was sin involved in the breakdown of their original union and subsequent marriage? Are they conscious of their sin and sorry for it? Did they remarry against the advice of fellow-Christians, and are they obdurate in justifying themselves? If there is doubt on these issues, then some kind of probation, with attendance at services without partaking of communion, may be advisable. But not for long, lest those concerned are turned away from the love of Jesus because they feel rejected by those who follow him.

Again, the church must decide, after prayer, and not the vicar or minister on his own. The church is one body, and everyone is a part of it (see I Cor 12:27). Of course, it is impractical for delicate decisions of this nature to be taken by an entire congregation, but small groups of caring folk can be established who can talk and pray together in pastoral situations, to seek and discern the mind of Christ. When a group makes a decision in this way, rather than an individual, responsibility is shared and the decision is unlikely to reflect personal views and prejudices.

Ministers and other leaders

Shortly before his death, while giving directions to Timothy about church order, Paul declared, 'The overseer must be above reproach, the husband of but one wife.' A deacon also, 'must be the husband of but one wife.' Similarly, 'no widow may be put on the list of widows unless she has had but one husband' (see I Tim 3:2,12; 5:9 margin). In the same way he told Titus, 'an elder must be blameless, the husband of but one wife' (Titus 1:6). Variant translations of his words indicate the problems Christians have had in understanding them. The New English Bible settles for, 'Our leader ... or bishop, must be ... faithful to his one wife,' and adds a marginal note, 'Or "married to one wife," or "married only once."'

Undoubtedly, Christian ministers and other leaders should be faithful to their married partners, and sexual misdemeanours should disqualify them from office. Equally, they should avoid polygamy, but in that they are no different from all other Christians. Is Paul then saying they should not remarry after divorce, nor indeed be men who have been married more than once, perhaps before they were converted. But if remarriage after divorce was forbidden in the early church, as Heth and Wenham have argued, why should Paul make a special point of denying it to elders and deacons?

Writing at the turn of the twentieth century, Alfred Plummer, Master of University College, Durham, insisted that Paul could only mean that ministers should not remarry after they had been widowed. Like Heth and Wenham, he produced supporting evidence from the Fathers to show that this was how they understood Paul's directions. He argued that in contemporary society, remarriage after being widowed was regarded as moral weakness. Since elders should be 'above reproach' they should therefore set an example to their fellow-Christians and to the wider pagan community.

Surprisingly, Plummer then proceeded to show that the rule was not universally observed in the early church and was frequently a matter of dispute. This led him to conclude that it was only temporary, like the recommendations of the Council of Jerusalem to abstain from various foods. In this way he was able to exonerate the Church of England in allowing widowed ministers to remarry, and thus, apprently, to achieve his main purpose![1]

In view of Paul's repeated insistence that death releases married people from their promises, and that when a husband dies a woman is free to marry anyone she wishes (Rom 7:1–3), it does seem strange that he should forbid remarriage in these circumstances to elders and deacons. Neither can the widow passage (I Tim 5:9) be called in support, for in the same breath he urges younger widows to marry, to have children, to manage their homes and to give the enemy no opportunity for slander (I Tim 5:14). Indeed, at a time when many women died much younger than they do today, in childbirth and shortly afterwards, remarriage for a widowed minister, perhaps with a young family to

[1] Alfred Plummer, *The Pastoral Epistles,* Chapter 11.

support, would seem highly desirable.

Unless we regard ministers as a class apart, bound to a higher standard of ethical behaviour than we expect from other Christians, we should beware of any teaching which leads in this direction. Christian leaders should set an example by the quality of their lives in every respect, and this is what Paul is saying in his directions to Timothy and Titus. In marriage, and in the upbringing of their families particularly, they should be above reproach. There is something inappropriate in a divorced and remarried minister, for his second marriage, however loving and honourable, will always reflect something of the failure of his first.

There is growing concern at the incidence of clergy marital breakdown at the present time, and at the frequency with which ministers in such circumstances are remarrying and continuing in ministry. The Church of England self-help group for divorced clergy wives, Broken Rites, is frequently incensed at the situations which are tolerated. This is not to deny that a clergyman or woman whose partner deserts them cannot continue in ministry, but perhaps they should consider their position very carefuly if they ever want to remarry. After all, there are many other fruitful ways of serving Christ within the fellowship of his church, apart from ministry.

Conclusion

Whatever principles we may follow in this difficult and delicate area, we must never forget that divorced and remarried people are among those for whom Jesus died. Many find, through the trauma of their divorce, that God comes to them in all his forgiving love and grace, and makes them his children through faith in Christ Jesus. In the same way, we must show his love to them, by accepting them as they are, and by assuring them that he can make all things new. Out of the ashes of broken lives can come something beautiful for God.

Marriage Encounter

A GROUP of married couples of all ages and stages sipped tea and munched biscuits nervously together in a small room in a Hertford-shire motel. Many were tired after driving several miles along traffic-choked roads and motorways in the late afternoon of a hot summer's day. Some were wondering why they were there at all. Some had been cajoled into going along, very reluctantly, by persistent friends, or nag-ging wives and husbands. All were uncertain, wondering what lay ahead. For this was Friday evening and the start of a Marriage Encounter weekend. For the next thirty-three hours with, so it would seem, scarcely time to eat and sleep, these fifteen couples would follow a concentrated programme of presentations and follow-up activities, out of which their marriages would emerge with new strength and com-mitment, with rekindled love, and for some, with the discovery for themselves of God's love in Christ.

Marriage Encounter was born in 1953 in Barcelona, Spain, when Mercedes and Jamie Ferrer called one day, to see a newly-ordained priest, Gabriel Calvo. Deeply committed Roman Catholic Christians, they longed to find a ministry among other Catholic couples whereby they could live out their marriage as they believed God intended they should. Soon they began a ministry which brought Papal recognition and blessing as many others joined them in proclaiming the good news of Christian marriage throughout Spain. Nine years later, Calvo organised and led the first residential weekend for married couples. So began a worldwide movement which Cardinal Suenens has described as one of the clearest demonstrations of the renewing work of the Holy Spirit in the church today.

By 1966, Marriage Encounter weekends had spread to South America; the following year they were started in the United States, both for Spanish and English speaking couples. Five years later, sepa-rate weekends were started for couples from Episcopal (Anglican) churches. Now, among many denominations, the movement continues to flourish in Spain and America, in Canada, the United Kingdom, Uganda, South Africa, Australia, New Zealand and other countries around the world. An estimated three million couples have experienced weekends since Gabriel Calvo pioneered them just 20 years ago. *Engaged Encounter, Family Encounter,* and *Youth Encounter Spirit*, represent newer developments and directions as Christians continue to reach out for the best in marriage and family life. In the USA, weekends for singles, for the widowed and divorced, and for those whose partners are in prison demonstrate the continuing vitality and growth of a vision now more than thirty years old.

In its Catholic expression Marriage Encounter extends to celibate priests and nuns, as well as to married couples. Since they believe they are married to the church by their vows of poverty, chastity and obedience, they explore that relationship, while their married brothers and sisters grow together in their own love.

Tea and biscuits finished, our 15 couples in Hertfordshire moved into another room to meet the team. Three married couples and an Anglican Franciscan led this particular weekend. Sometimes three couples will lead between them, but then one is always a clergyman and his wife. All had originally participated in weekends themselves and then, after further weekends and training, had been recognised as leaders. Working in teams of three and four the leaders gave presentations about different aspects of human personality and marriage. They demonstrated a technique of communication called Dialogue, and encouraged the participants to begin to practise Dialogue themselves. First, the couples separated, the husbands perhaps staying in the conference room while the wives returned to their own rooms, or maybe the other way round. Alone, they wrote to each other, honestly expressing their feelings about the presentation they had just seen or about suggested questions arising from it. Then together, in the privacy of their rooms, they read each other's letters and tried to understand their feelings by discussing them together.

Leaders of Marriage Encounter are understandably reluctant to disclose what happens on a residential weekend, since it is an experience to be enjoyed and not a process to be observed. Words are inadequate to convey the effect on a married couple when husband and wife devote 33 hours exclusively to each other, sharing their feelings on such subjects as money, sex, bereavement, and their response to God and affirming their love. In an amazing way the weekend meets each couple's individual needs; as they respond they find their love rekindled and the quality of their relationship immeasurably enhanced. 'It put the sparkle back into our married life,' said Tom and Jean, a couple in early middle life. 'We'd always been brought up not to show our feelings for each other, particularly when others were around. Now, when our adult children see us holding hands, or looking into each other's eyes they say, "Oh, you two, you're at it again!"'

When my wife and I went on our weekend we honestly wondered what could be in it for us. We had had our ups and downs like everyone else, but we had never stopped communicating, and we had worked through some pretty big problems together. For a year after we first met, we were apart for much of the time. During that time, we had gladly written to each other every day. Why had we stopped when we married? The discovery, on our weekend, that we could still write love letters, began to draw us together at a level we had rarely known before. Even though we had always been honest and open, we found we could say things through our letters which we could not say with our lips. After exchanging one particularly memorable pair of letters, we just burst into tears and fell into each other's arms. 'So did we,' confided another couple with whom we shared our experience.

This sharing of feelings within the affirmation of love is fundamental to effective communication. 'Feelings are neither right nor wrong; they just are,' is one of the Marriage Encounter's axioms. What we do with our feelings may be right or wrong, but they themselves are morally neutral. They describe our inner being as it is at this moment. We have nothing to lose by expressing them, but everything to gain.

'God does not make rubbish!' is another axiom. Most of us have a poor self-image, thinking more of our failures and inadequacies and weaknesses than of our strengths. In order to love effectively, we need to accept ourselves as we are, without always wishing we were someone else. We must compliment each other, rather than criticise, whenever we can. We need to know that God loves us, that he has made us for himself to reflect his image, and he does not make rubbish.

'Love is a decision, not a feeling.' The romantic traditions of films and television teach us to rely on our feelings in assessing and expressing love. So we fall in or out of love, and increasingly imagine we can change our partner whenever we feel like it. But love is a decision, not a feeling. Love goes on loving, even when it does not feel like loving. Love passes through a continuous cycle of romance, disillusionment and joy. Only as we keep on loving, do we pass through the disillusionment to the joy which lies ahead.

Marriage Encounter never expects participating couples to share their feelings with anyone other than themselves. Complete confidentiality is preserved throughout the weekend. The leadership team always includes a priest or ordained minister in case individuals or couples request additional specific help, but this is never forced. Apart from a nominal booking fee, weekends are offered without charge, although participants are invited to contribute towards the costs of subsequent weekends for other couples. All are welcome, whether or not they profess Christian commitment, the only requirement being that, however good they believe their marriage to be, they both desire something better. Indeed, in North America, Marriage Encounter is seen as a significant evangelistic force, bringing into the life of the church many who would not be there if they had not shared in a weekend. Christians or not, couples are not left to themselves once a conference has finished. Wherever possible, they are linked to a local Marriage Encounter group which is committed to providing support and encouragement.

Because of its heavy dependence on listening and writing, some find Marriage Encounter too word-orientated. With notes on the presentations and our letters to each other, we each filled an exercise book during our weekend; some couples went well into their second book. Although tape-recorders are supplied to blind or dyslexic participants, and special arrangements are made for the deaf, a weekend really demands a fairly high standard of literacy from those who attend if they are to get the best out of it. The movement's leaders are particularly sensitive to this criticism, pointing, in reply, to its working-class roots and its success in third world countries like Uganda. But some couples cannot respond to the concentrated programme of listening and writing which is expected, with only one brief hour for genuine relaxation on the Saturday afternoon; their weekend can become a nightmare, rather than a joyful awakening.

Nor is Marriage Encounter designed for couples with serious problems. Although miracles have occurred, its appeal is openly directed to those with good marriages. A good marriage is defined as one in which husband and wife are committed to each other and intend to stay together. Encounter's purpose is to improve the quality of existing relationships, rather than rescue and repair broken ones.

Nevertheless, Marriage Encounter represents one positive Christian approach to the present crisis. Although now established, it is still sufficiently in its infancy to point a way forward to Christians concerned at the tidal wave of marital unhappiness and breakdown which is causing such havoc in Western society. Marriage Review is another example of Christians acting together to enable themselves and others to realise and fulfil their wedding promises. Less dependent on words and more charismatic than Marriage Encounter, it includes ministry for healing of resentment, bitterness and inner wounds in its programme. So couples are helped to make their marriages work despite all the odds stacked against them, to dream the impossible dream, to express their love for each other in all its richness as long as they live.

CHAPTER 22

Marriage Repair

DAVID and Christine Mitchell live in Bristol, where David works as a solicitor. Inevitably, he sees a growing number of clients who ask him to arrange a divorce. Over the years, he has come to realise that this is not what many of them want, yet once they step inside his office they are somehow caught in an irresistible current which carries them to divorce, with all the trauma and heartache that follow.

English law works on an adversarial system, prosecutor versus accused, plaintiff versus defendant. In 1859, when divorce passed into the hands of the courts, the adversarial principle was applied: the claimant had to prove one of a number of matrimonial offences against the respondent. Since petitions had to be presented in court by lawyers who charged high fees, divorce, for long, was restricted to the rich, until, in the twentieth century, legal aid was granted to the poor.

The law has now abandoned the idea of matrimonial offence, but the claimant still has to prove that the marriage has 'irretrievably broken down.' The respondent can dispute this but rarely does so. Even if he or she succeeds, five years separation counts as irretrievable breakdown anyway, so the determined claimant can still have a divorce irrespective of the wishes of the other party. English law courts are now more concerned with arrangements for divorce: dividing property, settling maintenance levels and granting custody and access rights to parents, rather than with the granting of divorce itself.

So, one Monday morning, let us say, after a particularly bad weekend with her husband, Mrs Brown walks into a solicitor's office and says she wants a divorce. The junior partner who will almost certainly see her will probably not realise that Mrs Brown is using the solicitor as a weapon against her unreasonable husband. She wants to frighten him into mending his ways. She wants the solicitor to write him a stinking letter warning him of the dire consequences of his behaviour in the hope that this, at least, will bring him to heel.

But our junior partner is a lawyer, trained to represent his clients' interests in court. He is not a marriage guidance counsellor, nor has he been trained to understand the dynamics of the client-solicitor relationship. He may not realise what is really going on when Mrs Brown steps nervously, yet angrily into his office. He is also under pressure from his senior partners to keep the practice solvent. Solicitors' time costs money, therefore he must spend his time in a cost-effective way, and that does not include listening to clients pouring out their troubles.

Mrs Brown probably needs legal aid if she is going to press her petition in court. But under current regulations, the initial grant of aid only allows her solicitor to spend three hours' work on her case. If he needs more time, and therefore more aid, he has to justify the expense to the Legal Aid Department. So our junior partner had better get the divorce forms filled out during the initial interview, just in case they are needed later.

The juggernaut has started to roll. Mrs Brown wanted to threaten divorce as a weapon, but already the petition is filed, the process has started. She is now being carried along on an all but unstoppable tide. No one has asked her to pause and think. No one, not even our junior partner, has pointed out the alternatives: judicial separation, for example, with identical financial, custody and access arrangements without the final break being made, or less formal separation whereby the couple agrees to live apart with interim arrangements being settled between solicitors. No one at all has suggested reconciliation, offering Mrs and Mr Brown help in settling their quarrels and living more peaceably together.

For Mr Brown is probably nowhere near as bad as Mrs Brown has painted him. If she is fed up with his wayward behaviour, he is probably exasperated by her nagging and hysteria. Yet when he receives her solicitor's letter he is frightened and devastated. When he goes to see a solicitor in turn he is encouraged to let the divorce proceed, and to allow the solicitor to secure the best deal possible. If he insists on fighting the petition, an initial hearing will be arranged between him and Mrs Brown, with their solicitors, before a junior judge. If reconciliation cannot be achieved there, and the setting is hardly conducive, he will again be urged to allow the divorce to proceed. Divorce suits engender bitterness and bring out the worst in people, so even if the marriage had not broken down when Mrs Brown went to see a lawyer, the legal process will almost certainly finish it off.

David Mitchell's constant experience as a solicitor, of the trauma of divorce and the inadequacy of the law to encourage or effect reconciliation, led him and Christine to pray that God would show them how they could help couples with problems to find a different solution. In 1981 they learned that British Telecom could provide a service called 'subscriber group transfer' whereby, they were told, ten people could be linked through the same number. So they called a meeting of Christians and outlined their plans for a counselling service; integral to the scheme were ten volunteers willing to man a telephone on a rota basis to receive incoming calls.

At the end of the meeting they were delighted, yet rather puzzled, to receive only nine offers of help from potential volunteers, nevertheless, they decided to go ahead. The following day, they received a call from an apologetic and embarrassed official to say that only nine people could be accommodated on the subscriber group transfer system, not ten, as originally stated! David and Christine saw, in this call and the nine volunteers of the previous evening, God's confirmation that he was guiding them; Marriage Repair was born.

Four years later nine volunteers are still manning their telephones on a rota basis, ready to listen to distressed and desperate people who pluck up the courage to call for help. They listen, prayerfully and carefully, as troubles are poured out. They offer hope. There is always hope, even in the worst situations. They tell their callers they have a Christian faith, even though half the callers have no Church background whatever.

For many, the chance to unburden themselves to a stranger over a telephone is all they need. After their conversation they can see things in perspective and find their own solution. But some others need further help. The telephone contacts offer follow-up visits by trained counsellors. If the offer is accepted they try to match callers with counsellors according to age, social background, and so on.

Some 35 couples currently work as counsellors, seeking initially husband to husband, and wife to wife talks. Both sides need to talk without the other side there. The counsellors aim, eventually, to arrange a four-way interview between themselves and the couple. They are pledged never to give up on any marriage, however hopeless it may seem. They do not always succeed in mending broken marriages, but, as long as they can, they keep on trying.

Counsellors meet together in support groups every six weeks. They share their cases and sometimes seek expert help from psychiatrists, lawyers and others. Many sometimes feel swamped with the enormity of the problems they meet; others fall into the trap of thinking they know all the answers. They pray for each other and examine their own marriages. Being at the sharp end of ministry they can easily come under attack themselves.

Marriage Repair publicises its work through an attractively produced leaflet, *So You're Thinking About Divorce...* Illustrated by humourous cartoons, it points out some of the drawbacks of divorce and suggests alternatives: judicial separation, separation and reconciliation. It contrasts the vicious circle of a depressed and unwelcoming wife married to an unpleasant unhelpful husband, with the happy circle of couples who are thoughtful and loving, kind and welcoming. Then, through the telephone number, it offers help. These leaflets are spread around doctors' surgeries and solicitors' offices. They produce between seven and eight calls a week, of which two or three go on to further counselling. Not only have they seen couples reconciled and marriages repaired; in the process many of their contacts have found a living faith.

Marriage Repair, like Marriage Encounter, is run entirely by Christian volunteers. This is both its strength and its weakness. Because its counsellors are unpaid they are totally committed to its vision and its work. And undoubtedly they have shown a way in which Christians can respond positively to the marriage breakdown around them. On the other hand, their shoestring budget and limited resources are typical of the limited way in which the church as a whole so often tackles pressing social and spiritual problems. Recently English Christians happily and properly raised two million pounds to finance the visits of Billy Graham and Luis Palau to Mission England and Mission to London. Why then should the urgent task of marriage repair be left to handfuls of enthusiastic volunteers? Because it is less glamorous than big-name stadium evangelism? Because it requires patient commitment week after week, month after month, as opposed to the climax of three-month crusades? Because its rewards are unseen and unsung when compared to the spectacle of thousands publicly confessing faith in Christ?

Every Church of England diocese appoints a Board of Social Responsibility with a full-time clergyman as its chairman under the direct authority of the bishop. Similar committees exist in all the major free church denominations. Machinery therefore exists, funds are already in being, to train and support marriage repair teams throughout the length and breadth of the land, with the full backing and encouragement of recognised Christian leadership. After three-quarters of a century of deepening suspicion and apathy towards the Christian church by the great majority of British people, unchurched folk in their misery and despair are turning to the church again with a new openness and sense of expectancy; perhaps the Christian faith has something to offer after all.

Yet so often, initiatives like Marriage Encounter and Marriage Repair are regarded with suspicion and even hostility by the religious establishment. Is it because they are lay led? Do they challenge the comfortable assumptions of those who have made it in the ecclesiastical stakes? Do they threaten the well-oiled machinery of ecclesiastical administration turning in endless circles to service itself?

In Western society we are throwing away our Christian heritage of 1,500 years. Family life is crumbling around us. A generation is growing to maturity, never having known Christian standards of fidelity and constancy in marriage, and therefore with no model on which to base its own family life in the future. The task before us is urgent, to state and restate God's plan for married people in his world, to encourage married people to realise God's purpose of love in their lives, to heal the broken-hearted whose marriages are in a mess and to bind up their wounds. Shall we rise to the challenge, or like the North African Church of Cyprian and Augustine, shall we fall victims to the forces of moral decay and marital breakdown which are threatening to destroy us?

CHAPTER 23

Marriage and the Young

Marriage and revival

Secular and humanist ideas have so permeated Western society that few young people now grow to maturity expecting to come as virgins to their weddings, or to live with their husbands and wives for the rest of their lives. They have little understanding of the nature of love, or of their relationship to each other as married people. Dominated by self-ishness, they regard happiness as a right and they will follow their inner feelings anywhere in order to achieve it.

The early church of the New Testament period faced a similar crisis as it moved out of the comfortable assumptions and rigid rules of Jewish culture into the pagan and equally permissive Graeco-Roman society of the eastern Mediterranean. Yet within a generation Christians had turned the world upside down. In the heat of persecution they established an envied reputation for their love for each other. And through that love they transformed human marriage, raised the status of women from chattels and playthings to human beings with equal status to men, and established the dignity and value of children. They defied the might of an Empire bent on their destruction, and brought a dying neo-pagan Emperor to declare, 'Thou hast conquered, O Galilaean!'[1]

How did they do it? At one level they did not. Their phenomenal growth and influence was not their work but Another's. The Spirit poured out on the day of Pentecost was the divine agent who empo-wered and transformed them. And the same Spirit has continued to renew and strengthen the Church ever since, making it a powerful influence for good in society as a whole. When the Spirit comes in power, human hearts are changed. Love replaces selfishness, exploita-tion turns to respect. Men and women delight to obey God's law

[1] See F.J.Foakes-Jackson, *The History of the Christian Church*, p. 374.

instead of following their own sinful desires. And when this happens on revival scale, the rest of society is touched. Christian standards of behaviour are accepted and embraced by the populace as a whole, even if many remain individually disobedient.

In one sense, the history of the church is the history of revival. Decline and disintegration is followed by renewal and growth. Tertullian, Francis of Assisi, John Wycliffe, John Knox and John Wesley shine like beacons in the dark night of human wickedness and rebellion against God, men through whom God worked in revival power to touch the lives of millions. Countless lesser heroes bear witness to the Spirit's transforming work in the world. For a whole year, after the Welsh revival of 1904 and 1905, not a single criminal conviction was brought in a court of law throughout the entire country! What similar change must have taken place in the moral behaviour of its citizens. In the same way, the East African revival of the 1920s and 1930s raised the status of women, established Christian marriage across a slice of the continent, and prepared a community of men and women of integrity to withstand the horrors of the Mau Mau emergency and the degradation of Idi Amin's rule.

Christian marriage in Western society will only survive its present crisis as God revives his church once more. Only revival will ultimately change the outlook of the young, restoring their respect for each other, implanting a desire to live lives which are pure and holy in the eyes of God in heaven. Only revival will stem the heartache and moral corruption associated with easy divorce, contraception for the unmarried and abortion on demand. For revival we must pray. 'Revive thy church, O Lord!'

But while revival tarries, we must not shrink from our Christian duty. The early Christians were tireless in teaching Christian truth and encouraging Christian behaviour among their converts. Fearlessly, they set Christian standards against the easy-going attitudes of the world around them. In the same way, we need a comprehensive programme of instruction in marital behaviour which will cater for Christians of all ages from childhood to widowhood.

Marriage education

Marriage instruction begins in the home. There, the growing child absorbs from his parents the behaviour and standards they bring to their marriage. If they are faithful and loving, he will grow to be faithful and loving in turn. If the home is filled with tension, he will become tense in turn and will bring conflict to his own marriage when he grows up. Education by example is the most powerful form of marriage instruction a child will ever receive. It will far outweigh any subsequent teaching he may receive in later life. As we have already said, one of our problems today lies in the fact that more and more children come from one-parent families and broken homes. As a result, they have no proper model on which to build their own married lives. Is it any wonder they fail?

After the home, solid instruction in Christian sexual and marital standards must be given to our young people in their teens and early twenties. These are traumatic years for Christian parents, and for their growing children too. In their natural rebellion many youngsters need, for a time, to reject their parents' faith, in order to find a living faith for themselves. With some, their rebellion will be greater than others. In the process, they may make dreadful mistakes. Then they will need Christ's forgiveness and the forgiveness of all Christians when they return from their prodigal ways.

Ageing clergy will not necessarily be most effective with teenagers, but rather young adults of impeccable character and aglow with the Spirit who can teach by example as well as by precept. They must be unafraid to set Christ's standards before their charges, regardless of the derision they might encounter from being thought old-fashioned and out-of-date. Equally, they must answer and discuss, without shame and embarrassment, the frank and open questions they will arouse. Christ's loving forgiveness when we fail must always be presented alongside the high standards he demands from those who follow him, together with the power he gives, by his Spirit, to obey.

David and Joyce Huggett minister in central Nottingham to a large congregation which attracts many students from the city's university and colleges. Because they conduct many weddings, they have pioneered preparation courses for groups of couples who are planning to marry. Using techniques developed by Marriage Encounter and Marriage Review, they gather groups of six to a dozen couples in their large and spacious vicarage from Friday evening to Sunday. There they learn the basis of communication with each other, and face their attitudes to money, sex, work and family. For many, the Saturday evening is often a time of forgiveness and healing as together the couples face up to earlier failure and wrongdoing. To conduct these courses the Huggetts have trained married couples from their congregation. They find that engaged people are often more ready to listen to them than they might be to the minister and his wife. Thus, the spiritual gifts of several people are expressed, instead of being restricted to the clergy.

Not everyone will be able to follow the Huggetts' pattern, but it does show a positive way forward which others can adapt to their own situations. In some areas, for example, groups of churches can combine to provide courses, or encourage engaged couples to attend a course organised by a larger church nearby. Lay involvement, mutual trust and firm leadership will all be vital, combined with a loving concern to help young people put Christ at the centre of their married lives, to let him rule in their hearts and in their homes.

For married couples, anniversary gatherings can be arranged, when all couples married in a church in a given year can be encouraged to return for a service of thanksgiving and renewal of marriage vows. Newly-weds groups can be formed, groups for parents with young children or with teenagers, and groups for couples with ageing parents. These can meet and disband according to need. And always, in the continuing cycle of Christian instruction, marriage can take its proper place, with congregations being reminded of their unique privilege to reflect in their unions Christ's love for his church.

Happiness is not a right, but a gift from God, and it comes to those who are willing to obey him whatever the cost. True happiness is often rather different from the world's conception, consisting not so much in the satisfaction of our physical and emotional needs, as in the certainty that God is with us in all the joys and trials of life, and he will bring us to his eternal kingdom. Those who in Hebrews 11 quenched the fury of the flames, who were tortured and refused to be released, who faced jeers and flogging, who were stoned, sawn in two and put to death by the sword, who went about in sheepskins and goatskins, destitute, persecuted and ill-treated, could hardly be called happy, yet because they remained faithful to God and obedient to him, they received something which eludes those who live in constant search for happiness.

So it is with marriage. Those who come to it in purity, forgiven and cleansed from their past sins, who remain faithful to each other despite all difficulties until God takes one of them away and who draw on the resources of God's grace and the power of his Spirit to heal them, renew them and give them love for each other, eventually find a peace and a joy beyond description. This is the Christian hope. This is the prize which awaits those who live good lives in Christ Jesus. This is the revelation of the sons of God for which creation waits in eager expectation (see Rom 8:19). We offer this joy to all who enter marriage and we work and pray for its realisation in their lives.

CHAPTER 24

Towards Christian Discipline

Besides the transforming power of the Holy Spirit and solid, constant instruction in Christian living, the early church also established Christian standards of sexual and marital behaviour among its converts by fearless discipline of those who failed. 'It is actually reported that there is sexual immorality among you, and of a kind that does not occur even among pagans,' wrote Paul to the Corinthians: 'A man has his father's wife.[1] And you are proud! Shouldn't you rather have been filled with grief and have put out of your fellowship the man who did this? ... When you are assembled in the name of our Lord Jesus and I am with you in spirit, and the power of our Lord Jesus is present, hand this man over to Satan, so that the sinful nature may be destroyed and his spirit saved on the day of the Lord' (I Cor 5:1–5). And later, 'the punishment inflicted on him by the majority is sufficient for him. Now instead, you ought to forgive and comfort him, so that he will not be overwhelmed by excessive sorrow' (II Cor 2:6,7).

Spare the rod

The work of the Spirit in discipline is as important as his work in regeneration, yet is less understood. It is necessary, not only because our natural human weakness constantly exposes us to sexual temptation, but also because the Spirit's work in renewing us releases us to love. When we are born again we begin to love our married partners as God always intended. We also love our Christian brothers and sisters, because this is what Christ commands. Increasingly in today's church life, we rightly show our love in warm, affectionate, physical embraces, and unless we are very careful, our emotions can run away with us. Before we know where we are, we find ourselves becoming involved in deepening relationships with those to whom we are not married — relationships which transgress the Bible's commands to 'flee from sexual immorality' (I Cor 6:18). A deep and largely

[1] i.e. his step-mother.

unexplored connection exists between our spirituality and our sexuality. When one is aroused, so is the other. Paradoxically, the work of the Spirit in renewal can result in immorality, which is then openly justified, or guiltily hushed-up. Either way, deep hurt is caused to the body of Christ requiring the discipline of the Spirit.

In regeneration, the Spirit works as he wills. 'The wind blows wherever it pleases. You hear its sound, but you cannot tell where it comes from or where it is going. So it is with everyone born of the Spirit' (John 3:8). This secret, unexpected work of the Spirit in the lives of individuals is one of the most exciting aspects of his activity. He loves to choose the most unlikely and apparently unsuitable of people in which to display his grace. He loves to call the blackest sinners and deepest haters of Christ through whom he demonstrates his transforming power. Again and again, we are left open-mouthed in amazement at the Spirit's work in new birth.

But the Spirit's work in discipline is exercised through the Church. It is not secret and unexpected, but dependent on human obedience to the direction of Christ. Therefore, it is likely to be distorted by human failure and misunderstanding. Instead of bringing healing and restoration, it may leave offenders hurt and alienated. Because we are all children of our age and culture, our judgment may be affected more by our cultural norms than by the mind of the Spirit.

Sally was a British nurse working in a Nigerian mission hospital. One day she severely rebuked an orderly through whose negligence a patient had died. For this, she was called to account by the elders of the church and suspended from communion for six months for losing her temper. No action was taken against the orderly. In Nigerian eyes, losing one's temper is a greater sin than allowing a sick patient to die. In Britain, the reverse is the case.

Cultural background equally affects our judgment in moral and marital matters. The Corinthian converts found it hard to change their permissive behaviour, hence Paul's judgment about incest and his warnings against consorting with prostitutes. Styles of behaviour change. The harsh Puritanism of a former age has given way to the licence and abandon of the twentieth century. All this is reflected in the Church's attitude to discipline.

Discipline itself is currently out of favour in society at large. Laws have become corrective instead of punitive. Schools have abandoned corporal punishment. Prison regimes have been liberalised. Even in the armed forces, discipline is not what it was. In Sweden, parents are forbidden by law to smack their children.

Similarly, in the Church, discipline is out of favour. The accent is on forgiveness and acceptance rather than correction. This is good, unless it means that our Christian lifestyle is no different from the rest of the world's. This was the problem in Corinth, where it allowed them to tol-

142

erate behaviour 'that does not occur even among pagans' (I Cor 5:1).

Our dislike of discipline also carries with it the danger of over-reaction. Apostles of a new Puritanism are already stalking the land. Scarcely have we freed ourselves from our Victorian inhibitions before we are enmeshing ourselves in new restrictions. Some Christian leaders are applying the one-flesh principle to require couples who have slept together to marry, irrespective of other considerations. Someone else has decreed that young people should marry the first person they date. In some Canadian churches, young married couples who have indulged in sex-play before their wedding are required to make public confession of their sin. If they fail to do so, they are 'disfellowshipped' and the reason for their excommunication is announced in their absence.[1]

If discipline, therefore, is going to work, it has to spring from a determination to be obedient to Christ, and from the conscious activity of the presence of the Spirit in the life of the church. Before the Corinthians could expel the incestuous member they had to assemble 'in the name of our Lord Jesus,' and 'the power of our Lord Jesus' had to be present. Paul's spiritual presence would then be part of the process whereby the Church could be healed and the sinner forgiven (see I Cor 5:4,5). Paul was no autocrat laying down the law, but an apostle of Christ directing the church into the mind of Christ. Anything else would only have made the situation worse.

The Jesus way of discipline

Sally's Nigerian experience shows how we generally think of discipline in terms of punishment. She had lost her temper, so she was refused communion for six months to atone for her sin. Basil of Caesarea thought along similar lines with his prescription for adultery.[2] But discipline is not primarily punishment. A disciple is a follower: the purpose of discipline is to teach us to follow Jesus.

Jesus himself spells out the action his followers should take when one of them sins. We quote his words from the English Revised Version to bring out the force of the singular and plural pronouns 'thee' and 'you'.

> And if thy brother sin against thee, go, shew him his fault
> between thee and him alone: if he hear thee, thou hast
> gained thy brother. But if he hear thee not, take with thee
> one or two more, that in the mouth of two witnesses or
> three every word may be established. And if he refuse to

[1] See John White, *Flirting with the World*, p. 48.
[2] See above, p. 124.

143

hear them, tell it unto the church: and if he refuse to hear the church also, let him be unto thee as the Gentile and the publican. Verily I say unto you (plural), What things soever ye shall bind on earth shall be bound in heaven: and what things soever ye shall loose on earth shall be loosed in heaven. Again, I say unto you, that if two of you shall agree on earth as touching anything that they shall ask, it shall be done for them of my Father which is in heaven. For where two or three are gathered together in my name, there am I in the midst of them (Matt 18:15–20).

This is part of a longer section in which Matthew collects many of Jesus' sayings about the characteristics of those who belong to the Kingdom, those who form the new community of the church in the world. They measure greatness by childlike humility (verses 1–4). They are concerned for the weak and defenceless and accord them their true value (verses 5–14). Forgiveness is their hallmark, however often they are offended (verses 21,22). Deeply conscious of their own unworthiness, they rejoice in a loving Father who forgives them completely (verses 23–35).

The King has given his subjects the power to bind and loose, to remit and to forgive. In first century Judaism, this power belonged to the Pharisees, but Jesus declares his divine Sonship by giving it to his disciples.[1] Indeed, when they exercise this power they become 'the church,' the living body of which Christ himself is the head. What they decide on earth is ratified in heaven. When they meet in his name he is there among them. Verse 19 is not about answered prayer, as is commonly supposed, but about this process of binding and loosing, which Jesus gives to his disciples. When two or three Christians agree about a moral judgment and grant forgiveness to a brother who has sinned, it is done for them by the Father in heaven.

Therefore the followers of Jesus have the power and the responsibility to correct those who fall. As Paul also says, 'If someone is caught in a sin, you who are spiritual should restore him gently. But watch yourself, or you also may be tempted' (Gal 6:1).

Two of the oldest New Testament manuscripts, the Codex Sinaiticus and the Codex Vaticanus, omit the words 'against thee' in Matthew 18:15, showing that Jesus' directions apply to all sins, not just ones in which a believer is personally offended. 'If thy brother sin, go, shew him his fault between thee and him alone.'

'Brother, I've heard that you are having an affair. Is it true?' 'Sis-

[1] For an outstanding expository study of the whole passage, Matthew 18:15–20, see John Howard Yoder, *Binding and Loosing, Concern* Magazine, No. 14, February 1967.

ter, people are saying that you and your boyfriend are sleeping together. Are they right?' In the confidentiality of a one-to-one exchange, the offending Christian is likely to confess, forgiveness can be promised, repentance can be sought and restoration can be assured without the shame of public humiliation. 'If he hear thee, thou hast gained thy brother.' This is the purpose of correction, not to punish, but to gain one's brother. The directions are to every Christian, not to recognised Church leaders.

'But if he hear thee not, take with thee one or two more that in the mouth of two witnesses or three every word may be established.' Jesus uses an important Old Testament principle here that no-one should be convicted of crime without supporting evidence from witnesses (see Deut 19:15). It takes some doing for two or three Christians to go and confront another with wrongdoing, unless they are sure of their facts. Christians need protection against malicious gossip and exaggerated rumour, so Jesus says, be careful before you accuse a brother.

Still the aim is to 'gain thy brother.' Maybe the issue is not clear cut. Maybe others are involved as well. The offender may have been sinned against, as well as being guilty of sin himself. The witnesses may not at first agree on the necessary action to be taken. But conscious of Christ's presence in their midst, they will work for forgiveness and reconciliation among all concerned, without adding to the shame and hurt which may already have been caused. Strong words may need to be spoken, but if the brother is gained, then all is well.

Only if the witnesses agree together, and the offending brother rejects their appeal for repentance and reconciliation should his church be told. Even then, suspension, or exclusion from membership, is not the aim, but forgiveness and restoration. Too often the discipline process misfires because one person, say the vicar or the bishop, or a small group of people, the elders, pass judgment and tell the church, instead of sharing the problem first. Then people are left offended and embittered because they have been held up to public shame, instead of finding the free forgiveness which Christ always offers.

Practically, it is almost inconceivable that a Christian who is accused of sin, and who is convicted before witnesses, will agree to stand trial before the whole church unless he or she is convinced they have not been fairly heard, that factors in the situation need further explanation, or the witnesses are biased in their judgment. In all probability, an offending Christian will quietly leave, even if they take hurt and bitterness with them.

Should the church then be told what has happened? It may have to be. Rumour and gossip may spread. The offended Christian may give an incorrect account of events. He may try to join another group of Christians, before the issues which led to the breach are settled. So the record may have to be put straight. If the offender has refused the opportunity to explain himself to the Church, that must be clearly stated. The door must be left open for him to return. Everything possible should be done to avoid party spirit and division.

The usual method of discipline, as we have seen, is suspension from communion. Yet communion is the sacrament of forgiveness. A penitent Christian needs communion more than anything, to assure him that Christ has forgiven him and loves him still. If he has been publicly excluded, even for a time, he may be denied the certainty of forgiveness just when he most needs it. If we publicly excommunicate people we say, in effect, that communion is for good people and not bad ones. Yet the reverse is the case. We all come as sinners to share in the body and blood of Christ. Why should we exclude the adulterer and not the Christian who is nursing hatred in his heart? Public excommunication always creates a scandal, whether by a bishop in a sermon, or by a group of elders in a church meeting. And people always take sides as a result, because some feel a natural sympathy for the one held up to public shame.

Paul says, 'a man ought to examine himself before he eats of the bread and drinks of the cup. For anyone who eats and drinks without recognising the body and blood of the Lord eats and drinks judgment on himself' (I Cor 11:28,29). Certainly, Christians who are living in open sin ought not to come to communion, and we should spell out the consequences of their action to them if they do. But we must not tell them they cannot come. Only Christ can do that, through their conscience. The communion table is his, not ours, and he invites sinners to his feast.

The exclusion which Christ prescribes is not from communion but from fellowship: 'treat him as you would a pagan or a tax collector.' Paul agrees when he writes, 'You must not associate with anyone who calls himself a brother but is sexually immoral or greedy, an idolater or a slanderer, a drunkard or a swindler. With such a man do not even eat' (I Cor 5:11).

When the church assembles in the name of the Lord Jesus and his power is present (see I Cor 5:4), if an offending Christian then rejects a brother's pleadings, the agreement of witnesses and the church's judgment, then every member of that church has a duty to send him to Coventry until he repents. For the church is given the power to bind and to loose. Notice, how in the Matthew passage, the pronoun changes from singular to plural in verse 17: 'if *thy* brother sin against *thee* ... Verily I say unto *you*, What things soever *ye* shall bind on earth shall be bound in heaven.'

Problem areas

How far can we take this process, particularly where moral and marital offences are concerned? Adultery and fornication are obviously always wrong and action should follow whenever they are suspected. Divorced people starting a new relationship need sensitive and careful help. It may be right to encourage them, or, more probably, to caution them and advise them to wait. Single people, developing a relationship with an unbeliever, should be reminded of the Bible's clear teaching against their behaviour. Nevertheless, Christians married to unbelievers should always be welcomed into the life of the Church as the apostles' advice to them makes clear (see I Cor 7:12–16; I Pet 3:1–6).

In assessing our Christian behaviour Paul tells us to consider 'the weak.' In Corinth, some Christians were justifying their continued attendance at meals in pagan temples on the grounds that 'an idol is nothing at all in the world and that there is no God but one' (I Cor 8:4). But not all the new converts were sufficiently grounded in their faith to cope with this situation. So the liberty of some became a stumbling block to others. 'So this weak brother, for whom Christ died, is destroyed by your knowledge. When you sin against your brothers in this way and wound their weak conscience, you sin against Christ' (I Cor 8:11,12).

Does not the same principle apply in the whole field of human relations? Society now accepts that boyfriends and girlfriends sleep together before they marry, and use holidays and weekends together to this end. If Christian couples behave in this area like everyone else, even though they avoid transgressing Christ's commands, are they not likely to become a stumbling block to younger Christians, and a scandal to outsiders, who may be forgiven for drawing the wrong conclusions?

I believe a whole area of debate needs opening up here, both among young adult unmarried Christians themselves, and between them and an older generation of leaders who are bemused by what is happening and do not quite know what to do about it. Jesus calls us to deny ourselves, take up our cross and follow him (see Mark 8:34). This may mean giving up something that is rightfully ours for the benefit of others and the honour of his name. After all, many unmarried Christians in missionary work who are preparing to marry, have long avoided sleeping under the same roof, even in the home of a married couple, or holding hands together as they walk down the street, because of the wrong impression this gives to the people they have gone to serve. Is it perhaps time for western Christians, in our pagan society, to give up some of our hard-won liberty for the sake of Christ?

The nature of the Church

Exercising Christian discipline in Jesus' way may be the most difficult activity of the church's life. There is nothing worse than having to correct a Christian who has fallen into open sin. And if he is a much-loved and respected leader the process is all the more harrowing.

Jesus' way of discipline will only work in a church which has determined to be guided and led by his Spirit, to function as his body with himself as its head. In such a church, every member will look, not only to his own interests, but also to the interests of others. Each will display the mind of Christ, who did not consider equality with God something to be grasped, but made himself nothing, taking the very nature of a servant (see Phil 2:4–7). So they will serve one another, taking a towel, washing each others' feet. They will aim to love, as Christ has loved them.

Very few of our churches are like this. One way and another, they have become religious clubs with human rules, pecking orders and protected positions. Denominationally, many churches are multi-national organisations with career and salary structures indistinguishable from other secular bodies. Time and again, leaders who fail go uncorrected, leaving ordinary Christians bewildered and confused. Disciplinary procedures, such as they are, leave a sense of injustice and a nasty taste, because position and expediency count for more than loving correction and the forgiveness of Christ.

But the church is called to live by the Spirit and not to gratify the desires of the sinful nature. Nor are the acts of the sinful nature merely concerned with sexual failure: immorality, impurity and debauchery. Hatred, discord, jealously, fits of rage, selfish ambition, dissensions, factions and envy are included as well. Those who are led by the Spirit are not under the law, so rules and regulations do not feature prominently in their judgments. Instead, their lives reflect the fruit of the Spirit, love, joy, peace, patience, kindness, goodness, faithfulness, gentleness and self-control. Against such things there is no law (see Gal 5:14–23).

When Christians live like this, discipline is never punishment and only rarely correction. Rather, it is the continuing process of helping each other to be disciples, followers of Jesus Christ. Marriage breakdown is infrequent, because young people, and older ones alike, are encouraged to choose a suitable partner in the first place, and then receive the support of the fellowship to make their marriages true reflections of Christ's love for his church.

The Newberg Friends' Church has pioneered a method which is proving remarkably fruitful in this area. Those who are thinking of marriage are invited to share their hopes and feelings with a group of fellow-members who know them well. Together they meet for an evening of fellowship and prayer. Afterwards the group writes a report, recommending either that the couple proceed with the wedding, with the full blessing and support of the church, or that they wait, and make no further plans for the time being.[1]

Crucial to this process is the support of a loving, caring community. Of course it can be misunderstood and abused. Of course it can lead to a new tyranny in marriage matters, more severe than any ever exercised by overbearing parents arranging their children's unions without any regard to their personal feelings. And, at the end of the day, if wrong is not being done, the individuals concerned must be allowed to choose for themselves. Sometimes, like Luther, we have to stand alone and declare, 'Here I stand, I cannot do otherwise.'[2]

But where a church is determined to live by the Spirit, to be led and guided by him, where love is the hallmark of its life, then it can be a profound comfort to any couple to know that the joy of their romantic love is endorsed by those who are closest to them in the Christian community. If marriages are made in heaven, then their divine initiative should be obvious to the body of Christ on earth.

The great joy of this process lies in its suitability for first and subsequent marriages. Why should we only question divorced people before their weddings? Most couples whose marriages break down admit they should never have married in the first place. Have we therefore not a Christian duty, not only to repair broken unions, and to enrich those already in being, but to begin at the beginning, ensuring, under the direction of the Spirit active in the life of the Church, that those who marry do so, 'reverently, discreetly, advisedly, soberly, and in the fear of God?'[3]

[1] See Richard J. Foster, *Celebration of Discipline,* pp. 155–157.
[2] See Roland Bainton, *Here I Stand,* p. 185.
[3] *Book of Common Prayer, Solemnization of Matrimony.*

CHAPTER 25

The Salt of the Earth

'YOU are the salt of the earth,' said Jesus to his disciples (Matt 5:13), the overwhelming minority of people who submit to my rule and who protect and purify mankind from decay. 'You are the light of the world,' showing a dark and alienated world how to live as God intended (Matt 5:14). Therefore, we Christians must never be satisfied with preserving God's pattern for marriage within the church. We live in God's world. The whole of humanity belongs to him. His pattern for us is his pattern for everyone. We must not shrink from proclaiming the good news of Christian marriage to the world, and from working within our various social and national situations to make it easy, rather than difficult, for everyone everywhere to live in God's way.

Example and teaching

We begin by setting an example. We pray that, through the quality of our love and our fidelity towards each other, our marriages may be the envy of those around us. We should not initiate divorce. If we have to separate, we should remain single to allow for repentance and reconciliation. This is the church's historic position. There is no reason why we should change. If we are divorced, and then wish to marry again, we should only do so after careful thought, in total dependence on God to succeed where we failed before, and with the confident support of a loving Christian community. Ministers who are divorced should consider their position before they marry again. How can we set an example to the world if our leaders accommodate themselves to its standards?

In our teaching we must fearlessly uphold Christian standards of marital behaviour. Ordinary people still look to the church for moral guidance; if we speak with an uncertain voice they are left bewildered and confused. Bishop Robinson's assertion,[1] for example, in 1963, that, 'one cannot ... start from the position "sex relations before mar-

---

[1] John A.T. Robinson, *Honest to God,* p. 118.

riage" or "divorce" are wrong or sinful in themselves,' probably did more to advance the spread of the permissive society at a religious level than any other Christian pronouncement at the time. Seized on by the media and quoted out of context, Robinson's insistence on the primacy of love was ignored. In the popular mind, everyone was doing it now, and the church said it was all right.

Just because people will not always listen is no reason for compromise or silence. Those bold enough to proclaim God's truth have nearly always been in a minority, and often a despised one at that. God's word cuts like a knife. It touches man at the seat of his emotions. It exposes his sinful heart and it hurts (see Heb 4:12,13). But God's word also heals. It soothes and binds up our broken hearts. Twenty years on from *Honest to God* the permissive society still flourishes, but its casualties are increasingly finding forgiveness and wholeness within those forms of Christianity which stood firm on the clear teaching of God's word, and which Robinson, at the time, unwittingly did so much to undermine. Robinson was right. Love is paramount. But he was also wrong, for I cannot divorce my wife as an act of love, nor can I sleep with my girlfriend or anyone else to whom I am not married and say I truly love her. If I do sleep with her, I am using her, and am likely to cause her and myself emotional pain, if nothing else. Man has not come of age. He is still a child: spoiled and angry with his own sin and weakness, desperately afraid he will destroy himself with demonic technologies accelerating out of control.

The future may not be all that bleak. Today's children who are casualties of marital breakdown could well react against the easy divorce of contemporary society. But only if they are shown a different and a better way. Let us grasp the opportunity to proclaim to the world the good news of Jesus. With him we can enjoy life in all its fulness. By his Spirit, marriage can liberate and not enslave us. Children can be a blessing and not a curse. Families can be stable: an anchor in a turbulent world, laying a foundation for generations to come.

Hearts and minds

'I just had to make love to you tonight,' says a dazzlingly beautiful heroine to the stunningly handsome hero in the television soap opera. The fact that, in the story, they have previously been married and divorced, and now the hero is married to someone else, is neither here nor there. They just wanted to have sex together, so that made it all right. Millions of viewers across North America, including hundreds of thousands of children, watch along with millions more in Britain and in a score of countries across the world. The actors lie in bed together, gazing longingly into each other's eyes, communicating fulfilment and satisfaction from their fictitious behaviour. Public attitudes give their endless series prime time ratings and ensure maximum advertising revenue for the sponsoring companies.

Worldwide television and the content of many of its programmes must represent one of the most insidious and persistent attacks on the sanctity of sex and marriage in the world today. Comedy shows, serials, films and drama all depict characters entering into sex before marriage, having affairs, divorcing and remarrying with, apparently, little emotional harm to themselves or their children, and with nonchalant ease.

Once, some people might have seen an occasional play about adultery or divorce. Carefully and honestly written, it would have explored the emotional impact on the characters involved. Afterwards they would have had ample time to reflect on the drama and draw their own conclusions. Even in the heyday of the cinema, the most avid filmgoers rarely saw more than four films a week. Censorship largely ensured that the ideal of lifelong marriage was encouraged, that family life was sacred, and that the eternal triangle rarely involved more than harmless flirtation.

But television fills our screens and our minds night after night, week after week, year after year. Children, particularly, spend an average of 25 hours a week watching, teenagers only slightly fewer. If we constantly watch 'good' and prosperous and beautiful people falling into and out of bed, and into and out of marriage, without seemingly ever getting hurt, then we shall assume that this is the correct and proper way to behave. And if, in addition, we read in tabloid newspapers of the real life antics of the stars, who make fortunes out of their television work, we wistfully wish we were like them too.

Against this torrent of damaging propaganda Christians must act. Some will see their role in terms of crusade against the trends of the times. But negative protest only invites scorn and derision, even if a few notable victories are won along the way. We need a positive response. In our entertainment-orientated society we need Christian writers producing material of the highest quality which wins its place in the ratings on sheer merit, yet which reflects Christian values instead of the shifting sands of secularism. This is not to deny that adultery and divorce are not proper subjects for television drama, but it is to plead that they receive honest treatment instead of being glamorised and portrayed as normal.

A century ago, floods of cheap literature and popular music halls appealed to the baser side of human nature, just as television and video do today. In reply, Victorian Christians produced scores of moral tales showing a different way. We may smile at their prudery and sentimentality, but they represented a proper Christian response to harmful pressures in their time. In London, the Old Vic theatre was founded by Christians to provide wholesome entertainment for the masses who were being lured away to unsavoury productions in the music halls.

This kind of entertainment must appeal to the whole of society and not just to the Christian sub-culture. In itself, it will rarely produce conversions, but by reflecting Christian standards of love, faithfulness and purity in and out of marriage, it will subconsciously prepare people's hearts to respond to the Gospel when they hear it in other ways. We must meet the world on its own ground, and in Christ's strength we must overcome.

Christ and Caesar

Marriage is a creation ordinance; it was founded in the beginning by God for the health and well-being of society. When marriage suffers, society suffers. If marriage breaks down completely, the whole social order will crumble and disintegrate. Therefore, governments should be concerned for the stability of marriage and the strength of family life. While civil laws should regulate breakdown because of the hardness of men's hearts, they should also protect the idea of marriage as a life long union between one man and one woman. If they fail in this, then Christians should press for their amendment and improvement. Some may enter the political arena for this very purpose, just as William Wilberforce did to free the slaves.

Over the last twenty years, marriage and family law in the Western world have yielded to the pressure of the permissive society. As a result, families have been destroyed, children left desolate and men and women heartbroken as their partners have deserted them for someone else. In response, the Christian voice has been surprisingly silent. We may no longer be able to command the attention and compliance of society. But we should not shrink from proclaiming the inevitable results of permissive legislation in human misery and emotional damage.

Since marriages contracted before the age of twenty are far more likely to fail than those entered into at a later age, the law of parental consent for marriage should again be raised to twenty-one. In British society this has been the traditional age of majority. It served us well for hundreds of years when we were allowed to marry at fourteen and when our expected lifespan was much shorter than it is today. When people are going to be married to each other for longer than ever before, why should they be allowed to marry young without parental consent?

Unjust laws which favour the rich at the expense of the poor should also be revised. In the United Kingdom those who qualify for Supplementary Benefit are regarded as married if they live together and their single person's allowances are reduced accordingly. On the other hand, where the joint income of husband and wife rises above a certain level they receive greater tax concessions if they live together as two single or divorced people than they do if they are married. The old idea that the poor should be forced to behave while the rich may please themselves dies hard!

Granting divorce on the 'irretrievable breakdown of marriage' is good, as long as both partners believe this is so. But it should not allow divorce on demand, nor should it automatically allow remarriage; that nullifies the promise to be husband and wife together 'until death us do part.' The law, as it stands in England today, gives virtually no protection to a partner who does not believe that a marriage has irretrievably broken down, nor does it give the partners time to reconsider their action and possibly try again.

How people's minds would be concentrated if they could have only a judicial separation for five years before a divorce, or for as long as they were paying or receiving maintenance for their children! How much misery would be spared if alimony were automatically deducted at source from salaries and wages! How many broken marriages might be repaired if the law required a breathing space between the end of one marriage and the start of another!

Of course such changes would raise howls of protest from the permissive lobby. But easy divorce and instant remarriage have not made people happy. Rather, they have left a trail of misery in their wake. We have no right to happiness. If we think we have, we only display our basic selfishness. Life is what we make it, and we only become happy to the extent that we work for the happiness of others. Nor are we free to do as we please. When we marry we accept responsibility for the life of another, and if we have children, for their lives too. By its proper restraints, the law should help us to keep our promises, not make it easy for us to break them. When we fail it should give us time to repent and be reconciled. Those who remain married beyond the age of 50 often find they enter a new period of deep fulfilment, comparable to the thrill of their early romance, only far, far better. What a shame divorce and subsequent marriage are denying so many this satisfying experience!

Conclusion

Marriage was ordained of God in the beginning. It is a sacramental relationship reflecting the eternal love of the divine Trinity. It is a covenant, reflecting God's gracious union with his people, expressed in its richest form in Christ's self-giving love for his church. And it is a contract, between a man and a woman, to be husband and wife together until one of them dies.

Marriage was established for everyone everywhere. Because Christians live in union with Christ, they have the potential, more than any others, to live in marriage as God intended. Through example, through proclamation and through their influence in society, they must not shrink from displaying God's intention for marriage to the whole of humanity. For we live in God's world and he 'wants all men to be saved and to come to a knowledge of the truth' (I Tim 2:4).

A Prayer

LORD, our Father, we thank you for the relationship of marriage, whereby we reflect in our earthly lives the endless love of your eternal Being. We pray that in our lives together, you will so work in our hearts by your Spirit, that we may submit to one another out of reverence for Christ. We ask that husbands might love their wives as Christ loved his church and gave himself for her. We desire that wives might submit to their husbands as to the Lord. And we long that our children, growing in love, will embrace your love themselves and express it in their love for others.

For all who are married and who are hurting each other, we pray. Heal their wounds. Bind up their broken hearts. Give them your grace to forgive and to receive forgiveness in turn. Fill them with the peace of Jesus, and enable them to begin again, amid the tasteless dregs of marriage turned sour, to find and experience the joy of new life in him. For the deserted, separated and divorced we also pray, and for their children. Comfort them in their sorrow. Strengthen them with the consciousness of your presence. Fill them with hope, and grant that, out of the ashes of their wounded lives may come something beautiful for you.

Bibliographical Notes

This is by no means an exhaustive bibliography of the enormous range of literature, religious and secular, currently available on marriage and related issues. It simply lists specific sources quoted in the text, together with one or two other significant publications.

The Alternative Service Book, 1980, The, jointly published by Cambridge University Press, William Clowes (Publishers) Ltd, SPCK, England, 1980.
> The long-awaited comprehensive alternative to the Book of Common Prayer for use in the Church of England. *The Marriage Service* is particularly important, combining, as it does, all that is most familiar in the traditional wedding ceremony, with modern insights into the sacramental and psychological nature of marriage.

Bainton, Roland H., *Here I Stand*, Lion Books, Tring, Herts., England, 1978.
> Re-issue of the standard, modern biography of Martin Luther. Useful for its treatment of Luther's personal pilgrimage from celibacy to marriage, and his developing understanding of the Christian home as a school for character.

Bainton, Roland H., *Sex, Love and Marriage*, Fontana Books, William Collins, London, 1958.
> Sub-titled *A Christian Survey*. The author traces the development of Christian marriage from the earliest times to the present day, with particular emphasis on Martin Luther and the Reformation period.

ed. Bassett. W., *The Bond of Marriage*, University of Notre Dame Press, 1968.
> Modern Catholic symposium on the theology of marriage. Particularly useful for the contribution by Alexander Schmemann, *The Theological Tradition of the East*, on marriage in the Orthodox Church.

Baughen, Michael A., *Let marriage be held in honour*, All Souls' Papers, catalogue number C33/2b/ASP, All Souls' Church, Langham Place, London, 1979.
> Robust and positive sermon on marriage preached by the author who is now Bishop of Chester. Particularly good on sexual morality.

Book of Common Prayer, The, numerous editions.
> Appended to the Act of Uniformity, 1662, this remains the constitutive document of the Church of England. Its *Solemnization of Holy Matrimony*, with adaptations by the Free churches, became the standard form of marriage among Protestants throughout the English-speaking world for over 250 years, and continues to influence modern liturgies.

Bridge, Donald, *Spare the Rod and Spoil the Church*, MARC Europe, Bromley, 1985.
> A clarion call for the exercise of discipline in the contemporary church. Of

obvious relevance to pastoral situations which arise in areas of sexual behaviour and marital breakdown.

Calvin, John, *Institutes of the Christian Religion*, English translation by Henry Beveridge, two volumes, James Clarke, London, 1957.
First published in Basle, 1536, and progressively revised and expanded during the author's lifetime, the *Institutes* became the foundational theological statement of Reformed Christianity. Noteworthy for its denunciation of priestly celibacy (Book 4, chapter 12) and the sacramental nature of marriage (Book 4, chapter 19).

Christenson, Larry and Nordis, *The Christian Couple*, Kingsway Publications, Eastbourne, England, 1978.
Modern, popular American evangelical treatment of marriage. Noteworthy for its general hesitancy about contraception and its strong advocacy of the rhythm method.

Crowe, Philip, *The Remarriage Dilemma, Church Times*, London, 4 January 1985.
Sensitive treatment of practical problems which arise with the marriage of divorced people in church.

Dominian, Jack, *Christian Marriage*, Darton, Longman and Todd, London, 1967.

Dominian, Jack, *Marriage, Faith and Love*, Darton, Longman and Todd, London, 1981.
Just two of Jack Dominian's many outstanding books on marriage. A Roman Catholic and Consultant Psychiatrist at the Middlesex Hospital, London, the author describes the dynamic of contemporary Western marriage, analyses reasons for marital breakdown, and argues for the permanence of marriage if human growth is to realise its full potential.

Foakes-Jackson, F.J., *The History of the Christian Church*, George Allen and Unwin, London. First published 1891.
Many subsequent editions and reprintings.

Foster, Richard J., *Celebration of Discipline*, Harper and Row, New York, 1978, Hodder and Stoughton, London, 1980.
Modern bestseller encourging the exercise of traditional disciplines by twentieth-century Christians. Its chapter on corporate guidance suggests a controversial method whereby Christians may be encouraged or discouraged to proceed with marriage.

Fox, Robin, *Kinship and Marriage*, Penguin Books, 1967.
Sub-titled *An Anthropological Perspective*, the book examines differing marriage and kinship patterns among various tribal societies around the world. A useful reminder that Western marriage is not the only form of marriage, nor is it necessarily normal.

Health and Social Security, Department of, *Report of the Committe of Inquiry into Human Fertilisation and Embryology* (The Warnock Report), HMSO, London, 1984.

Heard, Grace, *Sex Before Marriage*, Letter to the Editor, *Church Times*, 23 March 1984.
A woman's testimony to the value of chastity before marriage and fidelity within marriage.

Henry, Matthew, *An Exposition of the Old and New Testament*, nine volumes, James Nisbet & Co., London, 1875.
Classic, late Puritan, devotional exposition of Scripture. Unforgettable for its comment on the creation of woman from one of man's ribs.

Heth, William A. and Wenham, Gordon J., *Jesus and Divorce*, Hodder and Stoughton, London, 1984.

A scholarly challenge to the traditional Protestant understanding of Jesus' divorce sayings from within the evangelical tradition. Required reading for all who really want to know what the Gospels mean and how we should apply their teaching, but not for the fainthearted!

Holloway, Richard, *Responding to the Sexual Revolution, Church Times*, London, 30 July 1982.

Huggett, Joyce, *Two into One?*, Inter-Varsity Press, Leicester, England, 1981.
Popular and practical approach to Christian marriage. Useful for engaged couples and newly-weds.

Ison, David, *Artificial Insemination by Donor*, Grove Books, Nottingham, England, 1983.
A sensitively written booklet on theological and practical issues occasioned by AID. Its final chapter, "A Positive Response to Infertility," is particularly helpful.

Jones, D. Gareth, *Brave New People*, Inter-Varsity Press, Leicester, England and Downers Grove, Illinois, 1984.
Scholarly, Christian analysis of ethical issues at the commencement of life from the Professor of Anatomy in the University of Otago, New Zealand. Withdrawn in the United States on account of its chapter on therapeutic abortion.

LaHaye, Tim and Beverly, *The Act of Marriage*, Zondervan Publishing House, Grand Rapids, Michigan, 1976.
Sensitive, well-written handbook on sexual behaviour for married Christians.

Marriage and the Church's Task, CIO Publishing, London, 1978.
The report of the General Synod Marriage Commission of the Church of England, recommending the marriage of divorced people in church in certain circumstances.

Marriage, Divorce and the Church (The Root Commission), SPCK, London, 1971.
A comprehensive Church of England report on the Christian doctrine of marriage which paved the way for *Marriage and the Church's Task*.

Matthew, D.J.A., *The Norman Conquest*, B.T. Batsford, London, 1966.
Exhaustive, historical treatment of England in the eleventh century, useful for its analysis of contemporary efforts to force Christian marriage on the whole population.

Morris, Desmond, *Manwatching*, Triad/Panther Books, Frogmore, St Albans, Herts., England, 1978.
Humanistic, illustrated, 'coffee-table' analysis of human behaviour from the author of *The Naked Ape*.

Paul VI, *Humanae Vitae*, English translation by Alan C. Clark and Geoffrey Crawford, Incorporated Catholic Truth Society, London, 1968.
Papal encyclical on 'the right ordering of the procreation of children.' Eloquent restatement of the traditional Roman Catholic condemnation of all forms of artificial birth control.

Personal Origins, CIO Publishing, London, 1985.
A Church of England response to the Warnock Report (see Health and Social Security, above).

Remsberg, Charles and Bonnie, *The case against living together*, Seventeen Magazine, USA, November 1977.
Interview with American sociologist Nancy Clatworthy about her ten-year study of couples who have lived together before marriage.

Rinzema, J., *The Sexual Revoluation*, English translation by Lewis Smedes, Chris-

tian Journals Ltd., Belfast, Great Britain, undated.
> Fascinating analysis of movements in European philosophical thought lead-
> ing to the permissive society.

Robinson, John A.T., *Honest to God*, SCM Press, London, 1963.
> Popular, best-selling liberal exposition of Christian belief from the then
> Bishop of Woolwich. Widely criticised on publication on account of its
> alleged compromising stance on sexual morality and divorce.

Sandford, John and Paula, *The Transformation of the Inner Man*, Bridge Publishing, Inc., South Plainfield, New Jersey, USA, 1982. Available in Great Britain from Valley Books Trust, Bulwark, Chepstow, Gwent.
> Excellent, comprehensive handbook for Christian counsellors written from
> an evangelical theological standpoint. Outstanding material on leaving and
> cleaving in marriage.

Schillebeeckx, E., *Marriage: Secular Reality and Saving Mystery*, English translation by N.D. Smith, three volumes, Sheed and Ward, London, 1963.
> Impressive doctrinal and historical treatment of marriage from a prominent
> Dutch liberal Roman Catholic theologian.

Search, Gay, *How to Survive Divorce*, Living Magazine, London, May 1983.

Steele, Paul E. and Ryrie, Charles C., *Meant to Last*, Victor Books, SP Publications, Inc., Wheaton, Illinois, USA, 1983.
> Popular and practical exposition of the thesis expounded in *Jesus and
> Divorce* (see Heth and Wenham above).

Stevenson, Kenneth, *Nuptial Blessing*, Alcuin Club/SPCK, London, 1982.
> Detailed, scholarly analysis of the priestly blessing in Christian marriage
> liturgies.

Trevelyan, Katharine, *Fool in Love*, Victor Gollancz, London, 1962.
> An autobiography.

Trobisch, Walter, *I Married You*, Inter-Varsity Press, Leicester, England, 1972.
> Fast-moving, popular exposition of Christian marriage, set in an African
> context.

Wenham, Gordon J., *Gospel Definitions of Adultery and Women's Rights, The
Expository Times* 95 (1984).
> One of Gordon Wenham's many articles advancing the thesis developed in
> *Jesus and Divorce* (see Heth and Wenham, above).

White, John, *Eros Defiled*, Inter-Varsity Press, Downers Grove, Ilinois, USA, and
Leicester, England, 1978.
> A sensitive treatment of Christian sexual morality.

White, John, *Flirting with the World*, Harold Shaw, Wheaton, Illinois, USA, and
Hodder and Stoughton, London, 1982.

Yoder, John Howard, *Binding and Loosing*, Concern Magazine, USA, February
1967.
> Detailed exposition of Matthew 18:15–20 with its implications for Christian
> discipline and the constitution of the Church from a leading Mennonite
> theologian.

Some Useful Addresses

For Counsellors and for Couples

Broken Rites, Pauline Morrell, Sec., 44 Van Don Court, Petty France, London
SW1
01-222 7291   Self-help group for divorced clergy wives.
Care and Counsel, 146 Queen Victoria Street, London EC4V 4BX
01-236 4970   Provides 2–3 day retreats at Highmoor Hall in Oxfordshire for
marriage enrichment. Preparation for marriage days for engaged couples.
Limited counselling available. Referrals to other local agencies.
Catholic Marriage Advisory Council (National Headquarters), 15 Lansdowne
Road, London W11 3AJ
01-727 0141   80 centres nationwide for marriage counselling and educational services: help to teachers, parents, youth groups, and school pupils in
understanding of personal relationships. Marriage preparation. Marriage
enrichment. Sexual and marital counselling.
Gingerbread, 35 Wellington Street, London WC2E 7BN
01-240 0953   Practical self-help and support group for one-parent families.
Westminster Pastoral Foundation and Association of Marriage Enrichment, 23
Kensington Square, London W8 5HN
01-937 6956   Training and supervision of counsellors. Help with emotional
problems.

For Counsellors

Association of Sexual and Marital Therapists, PO Box 62, Sheffield S10 3TS
Hon. Secretary F. Cooper. An association of trained members of the helping
professions involved in sexual and marital therapy.
British Association of Counselling, 37A Sheep Street, Rugby, Warwicks, CV21
3BX
0788 78328   A national association for those working as counsellors. The
Personal, Sexual, Marital, Family and Pastoral Care and Counselling Divi-
sions specialise in marital difficulties. Referrals to local individuals and agencies.
London Diocesan Board for Social Responsibility, London Diocesan House, 30
Causton Street, London SW1P 4AU
01-821 0950   Voluntary social work agency of the Church of England with
offices throughout London boroughs north of the Thames. Addresses of
local offices available from this number.
Marriage Education Panel, Church House, Dean's Yard, London SW1P 3NZ
01-222 9011   Education panel advising house of bishops and clergy of
Church of England on marriage.

For Couples

Citizens' Advice Bureaux—listed in all local telephone directories
    Trained counsellors provide free and impartial advice on all subjects, including marriage and family problems. Source of current information through network of specialists and experts in a variety of fields.
Family Planning Information Service, 27–35 Mortimer Street, London W1N 7RJ
    01-636 7866   Advice and information on all aspects of contraception, sexuality, personal relationships, and fertility. Referrals list. 1700 clinics nationwide.
Family Welfare Association, 501–505 Kingsland Road, Dalston London E8 4AU
    01-254 6251   Will provide information about local area offices nationwide.
Good News Crusade, 32A Fore Street, St Austell, Cornwall PL25 5EP
    0726 72716   Involved in biblically based marital counselling. Conferences held nationwide for couples, families and young people.
Institute of Marital Studies, Tavistock Centre, 120 Belsize Lane, London NW3
    01-435 7111   Therapy for those in relationship difficulties. Individual and group psychotherapy for adults and children.
Jewish Marriage Council, 23 Ravenshurst Avenue, London NW4 4EL
    01-203 6311   Confidential and professional counselling for single and married people and for families in all areas of relationships. Preventative counselling through group discussion, youth clubs, in-school instruction, classes for engaged couples and newlyweds.
London Marriage Guidance Council, 76A New Cavendish Street, London W1M 7LB
    01-580 1087   Offer counselling for all couples and single people in the area of relationships. General relationship counselling and sexual counselling.
Marriage Encounter, Anglican Expression: John and Sara Wheatley, 4 Hall Place Gardens, St Albans, Herts AL1 3SP
    0727 63183
    Baptist Expression: Bill and Brenda Reynolds, 26 Bellingdon Road, Chesham, Bucks HP5 2HA
    Catholic Expression: David and Pauline Perkins, 75 Station Road, West Horndon, Brentwood, Essex
    Offers weekends away for couples who wish to strengthen their marriages. Training in communication of shared hopes, dreams, frustrations, and fears. Open to couples of any faith or none; emphasis not on religious instruction but on the relationship between the couple.
Marriage Review, David and Joyce Connor, Woodham Mortimer House, Nr Maldon, Essex CM9 6SW.
National Marriage Guidance Council, Herbert Gray College, Little Church Street, Rugby, Warwicks CV21 3AP
    0788 73241   Referral advice to any part of the country, or consult your telephone directory for local branches.
The Samaritans, 39 Walbrook, London EC4 8BP
    01-283 3400   Offer themselves as carers and listeners to those facing trouble or crisis in marriage. See local telephone directory for your nearest branch.

Index